"As a regular speaker at men's conferences, I have a ⎯⎯⎯⎯⎯⎯
view of manhood that has crept into a Christian vie⎯⎯⎯⎯⎯⎯
are taught to model their lives after macho-styled wa⎯⎯⎯⎯⎯ ⎯rowing toward
a much higher form of strength, that of peacemakers. This is why I love *Living That
Matters*. This practical book shines as a beacon of light to guide men through the
stormy seas of toxic masculinity toward a more Jesus-centered ideal of what it means
to be a man."

—REV. COLIN MCCARTNEY, co-director of Connect City Ministries and author of
Let the Light In

"This handbook brilliantly weaves together quotes, stories, movies, plays, and so on
about a multitude of topics related to men—even the very challenging and uncomfortable ones. It combines a thorough grounding in scripture with highly credible
psychological and sociological insights. I don't know of another men's ministry book
that comes close to doing what this one does. Many in their twilight years wonder
whether their life has mattered. If you seek to be strong, loving, and wise—if you seek
to live a life that matters—this book, read in the company of a group of companions,
will get you there."

—DOUG KLASSEN, executive minister of Mennonite Church Canada

"Having known and listened to Steve Thomas for years, I—and many other people—
have experienced him as a man of true wisdom, in the best biblical tradition. It oozes
out of him in a visceral way that touches the soul and awakens what we already know,
but with greater clarity. Alongside Don Neufeld, Steve does it again in *Living That
Matters*, with deep and practical insights honed by his awareness of his own, and our
own, mortality. I strongly encourage searching and serious men to read and carefully reflect on his practical wisdom in this new book. Your life will expand with the
divine spark shared by Steve and Don."

—FR. ROBERT COLARESI, O. Carm., director of Carmelite Spiritual Center in Darien,
Illinois, and convener of Illuman of Illinois

"Steve Thomas and Don Neufeld's previous book helped us see what is destructive
about patriarchy and pointed toward a vision of healthy masculinity; now, *Living
That Matters* provides concrete and holistic ways to embody that vision. This second step is a crucial one. Like all domination systems, patriarchy is wily: it will find
ways for people to think the right thoughts without fundamentally changing their
attitudes and actions. This means that only a concrete set of practices, embedded in
ordinary lives, can bring about transformation. I hope that many men throughout
the church will take up the challenge presented by this book. Their own well-being,
as well as the well-being of everyone around them, depends on it."

—RACHEL MILLER JACOBS, associate professor of congregational formation at
Anabaptist Mennonite Biblical Seminary

"*Living That Matters* reminds me of an admonition I gave my children at the dinner table when they sat cockeyed in their chair, ready to go out for the evening: 'Sit straight in your chair and eat like you mean it.' With a tremendous resource of wisdom teaching, conversation starters, and all-important pauses for reflection, authors Steve Thomas and Don Neufeld call us to live like we mean it, ask the hard questions, participate in a circle of trusted companions, and work at becoming strong, loving, and wise men of God."

—**DAVID WENGER**, spiritual director and massage therapist at The Hermitage Retreat Center, Three Rivers, Michigan, and cofounder of IN-MI MALEs (Men as Learners and Elders), a chapter of Illuman

"*Living That Matters* is an outstanding resource that allows men to engage in various relevant topics relating to living faithfully and restoratively. Each section is thoughtfully written, with discussion questions bound to foster great conversations. I look forward to using this book as a resource for men in our peacebuilding work."

—**ROD FRIESEN**, restorative justice program coordinator for Mennonite Central Committee (MCC) Ontario

"As I near the second half of life, I am longing to be around men who know they're broken, and I am interested in resources that acknowledge the gifts and shadows that come with being a man. In *Living That Matters*, authors Steve Thomas and Don Neufeld give us a set of spiritual power tools to examine ourselves and have real talk about the wounds, challenges, and opportunities that men face on the journey to wholeness."

—**SHAWN CASSELBERRY**, author, global talent manager at Internal Family Systems Institute, and cofounder of Story Sanctum, an online shrine to sacred storytelling

"I'm convinced that the worthiest of goals is to become a good ancestor. The future of our planet and the realization of God's shalom may depend on it. Authors Steve Thomas and Don Neufeld have developed a road map to help men move in that direction while accompanying them on the journey of becoming more generative and wise. In a day and age when toxic masculinity runs amok, they offer an alternative vision that men of faith can embrace—a vision that involves community, contemplation, conversation, and faithful action. The result will lead not only to healthier masculinity for our times, but to a blessing for future generations, who will look back with gratitude."

—**JOEL BLUNK**, Presbyterian minister, spiritual director, retreat leader, and Illuman weaver

LIVING *that* MATTERS

LIVING *that* MATTERS

HONEST CONVERSATIONS *for* MEN *of* FAITH

Steve Thomas & Don Neufeld

HERALD
PRESS

Harrisonburg, Virginia

Herald Press
PO Box 866, Harrisonburg, Virginia 22803
www.HeraldPress.com

Library of Congress Cataloging-in-Publication Data
Names: Thomas, Steve, 1953- author. | Neufeld, Don, author.
Title: Living that matters : honest conversations for men of faith / Steve Thomas and Don Neufeld.
Description: Harrisonburg, Virginia : Herald Press, [2022] | Includes bibliographical references.
Identifiers: LCCN 2022042877 (print) | LCCN 2022042878 (ebook) | ISBN 9781513811956 (paperback) | ISBN 9781513811963 (ebook)
Subjects: LCSH: Christian men—Life skills guides. | Christian men—Conduct of life. | Masculinity—Religious aspects—Christianity. | BISAC: RELIGION / Christian Living / Men's Interests | SOCIAL SCIENCE / Gender Studies
Classification: LCC BV4528.2 T47 2022 (print) | LCC BV4528.2 (ebook) | DDC 248.8/42—dc23/eng/20221104
LC record available at https://lccn.loc.gov/2022042877
LC ebook record available at https://lccn.loc.gov/2022042878

Study guides are available for many Herald Press titles at www.HeraldPress.com.

LIVING THAT MATTERS
© 2023 by Herald Press, Harrisonburg, Virginia 22803. 800-245-7894. All rights reserved.
Library of Congress Control Number: 2022042877
International Standard Book Number: 978-1-5138-1195-6 (paperback); 978-1-5138-1196-3 (ebook)
Printed in United States of America
Cover and interior design by Merrill Miller
Cover photo by Mike Fitzpatrick/iStockphoto/Getty Images

27 26 25 24 23   10 9 8 7 6 5 4 3 2 1

We dedicate this book to a vision of men
embracing themselves as beloved sons of God;
respecting others as beloved children of God;
following Jesus, the image of God and model human;
partnering with marginalized people seeking justice;
protecting the earth as stewards of God's creation;
serving the mission of God's shalom on earth;
becoming strong, loving, and wise in the Spirit.

CONTENTS

FOREWORD

IN THE PAST HALF CENTURY, what it means to be a male in North American society has been undergoing an overhaul. Through this book's profound reflections on over seventy topics, Steve Thomas and Don Neufeld guide us through the new wilderness of manhood in the twenty-first century. Drawing on a wealth of resources from their decades in ministry and counseling, the authors open conversations for men to speak of their own experience, doubts, strengths, and longings. From such sharing together, friendships will deepen and individuals will find greater meaning in their relationships, work, spiritual life, and service to their communities.

Over the past sixty years, we have witnessed the civil rights movement of the 1960s and '70s and the women's movement of the 1970s and have entered a new era of mutual interaction among genders and races. The creative impulse of people of all genders, races, and ethnicities finding solutions together is much needed as we address global, local, and ecological concerns. The Anabaptist focus on peacemaking can contribute significantly to our global conversations.

My wife and I were married in 1967. Ruth remembers that as a woman she could not get a credit card in her own name at that time, unless she had a male cosigner—imagine! So yes, we are making headway in equality, in simple daily economic practices, in the workplace, in the church, in politics, business, and education, and in our homes and families. As men, we are learning to embrace gender and racial equality at all levels of life, work, and decision-making. As we enter this new era of mutuality, we have much to learn and contribute.

Living That Matters is a comprehensive guide for us as men to examine our faith, our vocational aspirations, our relationships, and our inner being. In this time of transition for all people in society, including men, we receive the wise counsel of Steve and Don. While crafted for men in the Anabaptist tradition, this guidebook is ecumenical in spirit and can be used by readers of all Christian traditions. For men unsure of their religious perspective, the book presents topics with an open spirit of interpretation of Christian themes. All men will discover fresh Christian perspectives for living lives of integrity, honesty, love, and devotion to our higher callings. *Living That Matters* is a marvelous resource for personal reflection, and when used as a guide for small group conversation, will open a depth of communication rarely achieved in such contexts.

I invite you to join Don and Steve on this amazing adventure into the depths of ourselves and into new forms of masculinity and community life.

—Rev. Dwight H. Judy, PhD
Professor emeritus of spiritual formation at Garrett-Evangelical Theological Seminary, retired United Methodist minister, spiritual director, and author of six books, including *Healing the Male Soul: Christianity and the Mythic Journey*

PREFACE

"YOU ARE GOING TO DIE." This was a truth Richard Rohr gave a group of us to ponder on a day of solitude in the desert during a five-day Men's Rites of Passage retreat in 2003. This reminded me of something I saw at Saint Catherine's Monastery at the base of Mount Sinai in Egypt: a room with hundreds of neatly stacked skulls from monks as a startling witness of eventual death. Based on dying and rising with Christ, this passage in the desert was a profound spiritual awakening for me.

Years after that transformative experience, as part of the Journey of Illumination, I did a death lodge ritual alone in the wilderness for three days. As I reflected again on "You are going to die," an invitation came to me: "So enjoy life." This invitation was based on what Jesus shared with his friends about living with abundant life and joy (John 10:10; 15:11).

Taking this truth and this call together, I placed these words next to a green man carving I have on the wall next to my bed: "You are going to die, so enjoy life."

These and other experiences have helped me face what's referred to as "dying before you die," as Jesus taught his followers, and thus to live with a greater awareness of the gifts of life and intention to live a life that matters.

This is more pressing for me now. After Don and I submitted the manuscript for this book to Herald Press, I had to face the truth of dying in a new way. After an emergency appendectomy followed by a colectomy, I was informed that I have a rare, high-grade appendiceal cancer. Suddenly, I realized that "you are going to die" may come much sooner than I thought.

Death puts life into perspective. Since my cancer diagnosis, I am even more aware of the gift of life than before. While it sounds like a cliché, I feel even more gratitude for the gifts of my family, friends, church, and faith. I well up with tears of sadness over losing these with the possibility of an early death. All of this transforms the depressive funk I occasionally experience that makes me question life. I now believe more than ever that life matters.

May the awareness of eventual death also help you realize that life matters. I invite you to wonder along with me: Knowing that I am going to die, how do I want to live? What really matters in life? And how do I live a life that matters?

As you ponder these and other questions in this resource, may you realize the call of Jesus to enjoy and extend God's abundant life. In your conversations with others using this book, Don and I invite you to seek living that matters and the joy of a life well lived.

—Steve Thomas

INTRODUCTION

DO YOU WONDER what it means to be a man? Do you want something more? Long for a life that matters? Seek to make a difference in the world? If so, *Living That Matters: Honest Conversations for Men of Faith* may be helpful for you or your group.

You're reading what's meant to be a practical handbook for men—a resource for engaging in honest conversation to deepen relationships with one another and God. It follows our previous book, *Peaceful at Heart: Anabaptist Reflections on Healthy Masculinity*, produced by Mennonite Men and the Institute of Mennonite Studies. That book presents Anabaptist reflections on being men—with a focus on following Jesus, forming community, and building peace—by sharing a model of masculinity that is more life-giving than today's dominant version of masculinity. All of this is set within our aim to live into God's shalom—a peaceable order with abundance, security, and justice for all, and well-being throughout creation. Our vision is for God's shalom to be established on earth as it is in heaven.

In *Living That Matters*, our intentions are to nurture life-giving expressions of healthy masculinity; address influences that undermine human well-being; call men to follow Jesus, who lived as God's model human; enable men to connect together at deep levels; and invite men to serve God's shalom in the world.

This book is not about men but rather a guide for men. Individuals may read it alone, but we hope it will be used in groups to engage men in conversation together. It offers more than seventy topics mapped into seven sections: (1) male formation, (2) human needs, (3) personal challenges, (4) sexual wholeness, (5) social practices, (6) conflict tools, and (7) life roles. Each reflection is a single, two-page spread that gets to the point and prompts conversation between men. Extra resources and exercises are included in the resources section at the back of the book and online at bit.ly/LivingThatMatters. Additional material may also be found in the extensive endnotes. While this book can be read in sequence from cover to cover, it's designed so the reader can easily turn to any topic of interest.

We pose hundreds of questions for conversation because questions can take people to new levels of relating. I (Steve) recall, for instance, late one night during my high school years when I was riding in a car with three other guys from our church youth group. We were joking about masturbating when I asked, "Hey, we joke around about this, but do any of us do this? I do." Dead silence. After a long pause, one by one each guy said, "I do, too." A simple question had opened up honest conversation about our shared humanity, which, in turn, gave us courage to be more vulnerable with each other. This deepened our sharing and our friendship. In the seven men's groups I've been part of and in the men's retreats I've led throughout the years, I've witnessed many men engaging in honest conversations that have enriched their relationships and spiritual growth. We trust that this will happen among men having conversations about topics in this book.

Don and I have written this guidebook in our roles as coordinators of the organization Mennonite Men in Canada and the United States, respectively. Don has worked as a clinical social worker and counselor with men for thirty years, and I have served as a pastor for thirty-three years, with many of these years focused on men's inner work. We acknowledge that both of us are white, middle-class, cisgender, heterosexual, able-bodied men raised in an Anabaptist Christian tradition and writing out of a North American context. We are growing, however, in our awareness of how we benefit from the power and privilege these identities give us while others are denied such power and privilege in their lives. Don and I recognize that our leadership roles and getting to write this book arise from power and privilege we've been given.

We have tried to build on our work in *Peaceful at Heart*, which engaged a diversity of men—Asian, Black, Indigenous, Latino, and gay—to paint a picture of the different experiences and perspectives of men. Still, we cannot pretend to understand and speak to all men's experiences and contexts. Also, more needs to be written on the experience of nonbinary persons in relation to men and masculinity. We hope this handbook inspires others to create resources out of their own cultures and in their own languages to encourage authentic conversations around gender.

In this book we talk about social problems from within a positive framework. We promote what we're for rather than just condemning what we're against. Take sexism, for instance. To transform patriarchy, we focus on God's shalom, which calls us to build respect, equity, and justice for all genders. While dismantling is part of constructive work, we want to cast a vision of God's shalom and to practice its values for changing ourselves and society. The "appreciative inquiry" model for social change states that what we focus on becomes our reality. Since focusing on problems may make them grow bigger, we instead focus on actions to bring about shalom. As we do this, we call forth health and positive change.[1] Think of this as remodeling—replacing something old and dysfunctional with a better structure for all people. Remodeling also speaks to our need for new role models for being men.

Reinhold Niebuhr, in his classic journal *Leaves from the Notebook of a Tamed Cynic*, writes about warrior prophets whose hard-nosed preaching about social problems caused people to resist change rather than pursue it. As a pastor seeking social change in Detroit, Niebuhr called for leaders to be less like scolding warrior prophets and more like wise statespersons who encourage people while calling for action. He believed that change in the world happens more effectively by inspiring people to act out of the goodness of their hearts rather than from a sense of duty. He writes:

On the whole, people do not achieve great moral heights out of a sense of duty. You may be able to compel them to maintain certain minimum standards by pressing duty, but the highest moral and spiritual achievements depend not upon a push but upon a pull. The language of aspiration rather than that of criticism and command is the proper pulpit language. Of course it has its limitations. In every congregation there are a few perverse sinners who can go into emotional ecstasies about the "City of God" and yet not see how they are helping to make their city a hell-hole.[2]

We assume that we're writing not to "perverse sinners" but to common men like ourselves who seek God's peace in our world and who prefer to be encouraged rather than scolded to change. With Niebuhr, we believe we're more likely to transform our lives and the world by being drawn toward the vision of God's shalom.

We hope this book helps men engage issues in their lives. Biblical scholar Patrick Arnold observed in 1991 that men were seeking to address a host of issues that affect human well-being:

Statistics show that American men are stressed out. Compared to women, they die much earlier, suffer higher rates of suicide, fatal illnesses, and substance abuse, and are more likely to be murdered, robbed, and assaulted; some scholars say that black men in America are becoming an endangered species. . . .

Men and masculinity are beginning to break down. This fact is of great concern to our whole society since most of our major cultural problems relate in some way to the collapse of masculinity: homelessness, crime, drug addiction, divorce, single-parent families, gang warfare, and so on. On an individual level, many men are also beginning to recognize the masculine spiritual crisis in their own lives in the form of father-wounds, alienation, emptiness in their work, collapsed relationships, and loneliness, to name a few. In the last few generations, these problems have grown too serious to deny or dismiss with a macho shrug of the shoulders. Men are beginning to face their challenges squarely.[3]

What Arnold saw then is still true today. It's also true that men want to transform these problems and live a life of greater wholeness, meaning, purpose, love, and peace.

+ + +

When I first thought about this book, three words came to mind: *strong, loving*, and *wise*—from 2 Timothy 1:7, where we read that God has given us the Spirit, which makes us strong, loving, and wise. Taking these words as the marks of a healthy, mature person, we offer the following reflections on these terms in reference to masculinity:

Strong

The original Greek word used in this text is *dunamis*, a root word for "power." Males are socialized to be strong, and in our patriarchal culture, men are given power. There's nothing inherently wrong with being strong or having power. The concern is what we do with our strength or power and how our actions affect others and the world for good or for ill. How we gain our power and how we and our social systems deny people power can become the root of serious problems.

Men are rightly criticized when they abuse power, using it to control, dominate, or violate others. Too many men use power over and against others, whereas we are called to use our power with and for others. What matters is not muscular strength but moral strength.

Consider Jesus as our model. He was strong—speaking truth to power, confronting evil, and calling for justice. But he used his power with and for others. Rather than lording it over others, he served them in his strength and with his love. This brings us to our second trait—loving.

Loving

The Greek word here refers to agape—unconditional, compassionate, and sacrificial love. We believe God is love and that we are called to live in and live out this love. Jesus says all the commandments hang on the great commandment to love God and our neighbors as ourselves (Matthew 22:35–40). This is the heart of it all—to love as God loves. This love is a matter both of the heart and of action. Lest we think that love is simply what we feel, we name that it matters what we do and how we live with others, sharing of ourselves and our resources. Jesus modeled extraordinary love, especially for the marginalized and the outcast.

Consider his tender, compassionate love for the poor, broken, and untouchable. Think of Jesus' gentle love with Mary and Martha and his tough love with religious leaders and his disciples.

Jesus said his followers and friends would be known by love. As a young follower of Jesus, I wanted to grow in love. I used to carry a card in my calendar with a self-test I had created from Paul's word list describing love in 1 Corinthians 13. To test how loving I was, I would substitute *I* for *love*, then read: "I am patient; I am kind; I am not envious or boastful or arrogant or rude; I do not insist on my own way; I am not irritable or resentful . . ." When I read this, I was reminded how much I needed to grow in love. I don't need this list anymore. Being a husband and father helps me realize how short I fall in loving like Jesus, and that growing in love is a lifelong process!

Strength and love need to be held together. Committed as he was to agape, Martin Luther King Jr. wrote that ethical appeals "must be undergirded by some form of constructive power." Power and love are not opposites, as often thought, where "love is identified with a resignation of power, and power with a denial of love." Instead, "what is needed is a realization that power without love is reckless and abusive, and love without power is sentimental and anemic. Power at its best is love implementing the demands of justice, and justice at its best is power correcting everything that stands against love."[4] We are to be both strong and loving. Knowing how to exercise love and power requires us to be wise—our third trait.

Wise

The Greek word here is *sophronismos*—which means to be wise with a sound mind, or to have self-control acting with good judgment. Knowledge must translate from head to heart, hands, and feet in order to be true wisdom. Our daily news too often shows what it looks like when men act without wisdom. The Old Testament highly values wisdom, claiming it as a crowning virtue for mature people of God living a good and right life. In the New Testament, Luke writes that the young Jesus "grew and became strong, filled with wisdom, and the favor of God was upon him" (2:40).

Paul calls us to live in the way of Jesus and his wisdom. In his letter to the Ephesians, he states that as we mature in Christ, wisdom will guide us in living a full life (3:14–21, 4:13).

Wisdom guides us in responding to anger, lust, greed, conflict, demands, and dilemmas that are part of our everyday life. As we mature, we hopefully grow in wisdom, giving way not just to aging but to "saging," where we become wise elders, serving as mentors and offering guidance for the next generations.

I think again of Martin Luther King Jr. and of Congressman John Lewis, who, out of Christian faith, exemplify what it looks like to be strong, loving, and wise. Both of these men stood in sharp contrast to fear, hate, and bigotry and to the toxic masculinity we still witness today.

King said, "The ultimate measure of a man is not where he stands in moments of comfort and convenience but where he stands at times of challenge and controversy. The true neighbor will risk his position, his prestige, and even his life for the welfare of others."[5] Amid violent racism, King showed what he was made of as he stood strong, claimed the power of love, and led with wisdom. He demonstrated this when put to an extreme test. After his home was bombed, his civil rights colleagues thought violence against them had gone far enough, so they made plans to retaliate. But King refused the way of violence and held instead to the power of love. "Returning hate for hate multiplies hate, adding deeper darkness to a night already devoid of stars," he wrote. "Darkness cannot drive out darkness; only light can do that. Hate cannot drive out hate, only love can do that. Hate multiplies hate, violence multiplies violence, and toughness multiplies toughness in a descending spiral of destruction."[6]

He further said, "Sooner or later all the people of the world will have to discover a way to live together in peace, . . . a method which rejects revenge, aggression and retaliation. The foundation of such a method is love."[7] To many, this may not have seemed like a strong, "manly" response. But King's way of being strong, loving, and wise proved to be a powerful force in transforming violence.

King's colleague John Lewis, who went on to be a longtime US representative, also lived out this spirit of nonviolence in the midst of being repeatedly brutalized and imprisoned because of his work for freedom, peace, and justice. On Bloody Sunday in Selma, Alabama, he suffered a fractured skull when state troopers attacked him. Despite this, he maintained an inner moral strength with courage, compassion, and perseverance. The call, he said, in the face of hate and hostility is to hold no malice in our heart but to have a heart of compassion. There is no technique or strategy to do this, he stated. Rather, it's a way and spirit of living. "You carry this love, this peace, this capacity for compassion, inside yourself every waking minute of the day."[8]

It's a love, as Lewis described, that "accepts and embraces the hateful and the hurtful. It is a love that recognizes the spark of the divine in each of us, even in those who would raise their hand against us, those we might call our enemy. This sense of love realizes that emotions of the moment and constantly shifting circumstances can cloud that divine spark. Pain, ugliness and fear can cover it over, turning a person toward anger and hate."[9] Lewis recognized the divine image in the other as a basis for practicing love.

William Gladstone, nineteenth-century prime minister of the United Kingdom, said, "We look forward to the time when the power of love will replace the love of power, then will our world know the blessings of peace." Men like

King and Lewis who exchange the love of power with the power of love bring about God's peace.

As we become strong, loving, and wise, our gendered distinctions diminish. All genders become more alike than different, reflecting our true selves in the image of God. We end up with a healthy personhood for a whole new humanity.

I wish for all men what my spouse Linda and I prayed for our children each night. At the end of every bedtime prayer with them, we closed with these words: "May they know who they are as your beloved children and be filled with your Spirit, who makes them strong, loving, and wise." We sought to imprint these words in their hearts and minds. Our daughter took this a step further by tattooing "strong, loving, and wise" on her body.

I look to the day when men embrace who they are and are known by these marks as they embody and extend God's shalom.

AN OVERVIEW OF THIS BOOK

SECTION 1 invites us to reflect on our experience of God, Jesus, and the Spirit, then turns to how our identity, gender, purpose, values, and practices shape us. We also look at how community, friendship, and service form us.

SECTION 2 identifies human needs. We look at the core needs of security, action, connectedness, recognition, and meaning in our lives and how these fundamental needs may be met in healthy ways.

SECTION 3 addresses personal challenges that men experience. These include grief, failure, shame, pride, anxiety, anger, greed, vulnerability, empathy, prejudice, and compulsions.

SECTION 4 discusses matters of sexual wholeness. We define sexuality, then consider embodiment, eros, integrity, confession, and vision. We also address issues of sexual orientation, identities, intimacy, and fidelity.

SECTION 5 identifies ten social practices to establish God's shalom. These are respect, compassion, inclusion, mutuality, freedom, equity, justice, diversity, sustainability, and love.

SECTION 6 looks at tools for making peace with conflicts in our lives. For this, we discuss conflict, power, and postures in peacemaking. We then examine the practices of nonviolence, courage, self-control, listening, and speaking. We map five styles of response to conflict and outline a model for collaboration.

SECTION 7 wraps things up with a look at the life roles we serve. The dozen we address are our roles as sons, brothers, friends, lovers, partners, fathers, mentors, workers, leaders, stewards, activists, and elders.

HOW TO USE THIS BOOK

in a Group Context

FIRST, before beginning a group, consider taking a full day or weekend retreat together with potential members of the group. Don or I are available to come to your area in person or virtually to help kick off a retreat on themes in this book. Or you might provide a retreat at the end of your group experience as a way to invite other men to join or form a group to use this book. (If interested in this, you may connect with Don or me via the contact information provided on the author bio page.)

SECOND, browse this book to become familiar with its contents, then discuss your group's interests and the issues you want to address. Consider how many sessions your group would like to hold and select sections for conversations together. Form a group experience that fits what your members want. If your group is new, consider having everyone tell their life story as described in the first exercise (see "Experiences" in the Male Formation section). Personal story-telling will deepen sharing, build trust, and form community.

THIRD, as you get started, consider making an agreement with one another about when the group will meet, how long the meetings will be, the duration of the group, who will facilitate, and expectations for participation. Anticipate that once your group reaches its scheduled end point, it might choose to continue after evaluating next steps—while also giving individuals the chance to opt out. For example, your group might decide to do one or two sections, then stop to consider whether or how to continue and what to discuss next. It's important to have clear and specific understandings on these points.

FOURTH, have conversations that matter. We invite readers—as they are ready—to go deeper in conversation than they often do by "getting out of their heads" and sharing their experiences with others. So, questions for conversation under each topic call for men to talk about their lived experience and not just what they think. For this, consider the following practices and any others your group adds, then make a commitment together to honor these:

- Uphold confidentiality to create a safe space.
- Share when you are ready to do so.
- Be vulnerable in sharing personal experiences.
- Listen with empathy and without judgment.
- Manage sharing so all have equal opportunity.
- Show love and respect for one another.

To experience deeper connections than we often have, we need to risk being vulnerable. While this may be challenging for many men because of what we are taught, sharing our difficult experiences bond us. As Ernest Kurtz observes in *The Spirituality of Imperfection*, "Human beings connect with each other most healingly, most healthily, not on the basis of common strengths, but in the reality of their shared weaknesses." This helps form community.

As stated, it's important that people share only when ready to do so. We need to give each other the freedom and space for this even as we stretch toward being vulnerable with one another. There's a time for holding things in our heart like Mary until it's time to speak (Luke 2:19), and there's a time for speaking from the heart like Paul when he openly shared his struggle (Romans 7:14–20).

FIFTH, consider the following points before and during your meetings:

- Read the single spread (left and right pages) topic sheet before meeting.
- Use the discussion questions and artwork to prompt conversation.
- Consider doing an exercise from the resources section, if provided.
- Follow the agreed-upon practices for group conversation.
- End by praying together.
- Close with the following words or other words of your choosing: "God, as your beloved sons following Jesus, make us strong, loving, and wise in your Spirit. Amen."

SIXTH, after completing each section, we recommend that the group pause to reflect on and discuss what you are experiencing in your conversations. Hopefully this space will offer love, increase your understanding, deepen your relationships, and expand your awareness of God.

Be aware that where two or three are gathered there is Christ, and there is often conflict. Honest discussions may surface differences, trigger emotions, and create tensions or conflicts in your relationships. To manage these for growth, we invite you to pay attention to what's happening between one another and how the Spirit is working among you. If this becomes difficult, consider how to address this together.* Having healthy conversations provides an opportunity to become more strong, loving, and wise. For it takes strength to speak our truth, love to respect each other, and wisdom to deal with our differences.

---

* Individuals using these materials and leaders who are working with groups should anticipate intense responses, emotionally and intellectually, that will need empathic and supportive responses. Be alert to individual and group processes that signal such developments, such as distancing and uncharacteristic silence or escalating frustrations and even overt anger. Offer time and space to process—while agreeing to the expectation that individuals who leave a meeting early will first touch base with the leader. Develop contingency plans for offering support, such as via a co-leader, both at the time the situation arises and by following up in subsequent hours or days.

ACKNOWLEDGMENTS

WE GRATEFULLY ACKNOWLEDGE the following organizations for their contributions that made this publication possible: the Schowalter Foundation of North Newton, Kansas; Shantz Mennonite Church of Baden, Ontario; and Mennonite Men of Mennonite Church Canada and Mennonite Church USA.

We thank Heidi King and the team of Herald Press for their wise editorial guidance, Merrill Miller for his creative design work, and Matt Veith for early contributions to the layout. I (Steve) acknowledge close friends, men's groups, spiritual directors, and the brothers of the Indiana/Michigan MALEs chapter of Illuman, who have been important companions in men's work. Both Don and I have learned much in our roles as fathers, and we thank our children for what they have taught us. Most of all, we are grateful to Gayle Neufeld and Linda Lehman Thomas, respectively, with whom we seek strength, love, and wisdom in marriage and life.

Male Formation

In This Section

Experiences

God

Jesus

Spirit

Identity

Gender

Purpose

Values

Practices

Community

Friendship

Service

INTRODUCTION

Steve

> *Abide in me as I abide in you. . . .*
> *Love one another as I have loved you.*
> **—Jesus, John 15:4, 12**

IN THE SECOND ACCOUNT of creation in Genesis, we read that God "fashioned an earth creature out of the clay of the earth, and blew into its nostrils the breath of life. And the earth creature became a living being" (Genesis 2:7 *The Inclusive Bible*).[1]

This forming of the first humans from the earth or clay by gods is a common feature of creation stories of the ancient Near East. In Sumerian mythology, humans are created from clay and blood. In Egyptian stories, a god creates humans from clay before placing them in their mother's womb. And in Greek mythology, Prometheus molds humans from water and earth. Although these stories have slightly different twists, in each of them humans are deliberately formed from the earth with divine intention.

The Anabaptist faith tradition holds that we not only were created by God's hands from the beginning but also continue to be like "clay in the potter's hand," fashioned into something good (Jeremiah 18:6). And even though we may be humble, fallible, and broken works of clay, we always bear within us the glory of God (2 Corinthians 4:7).

That we are fashioned from clay suggests we are malleable—readily formed by life. In this section on male formation, we examine a dozen factors that form us as men.

The first section focuses on experiences that shape our lives. We recommend that groups start by learning to know one another more deeply through each person sharing their story as suggested in the exercise. We provide a list of formative life experiences and questions for conversation.

For many if not most men, this may be the first time recounting your life story and how it has formed the kind of person you've become. We encourage groups to take time for personal storytelling before proceeding with the next topics. This is a way to form community and build trust for conversations to follow.

After storytelling about our life experiences, we turn to our faith and spiritual experience. We begin with God, the One who breathes life into our being. We examine images we have of God and discuss God's unconditional healing love for us. We then turn to Jesus, who reveals in the flesh what God is like, the way of love, and how to be fully human. After Jesus, we focus on the Spirit as God's transforming presence and power. We consider the work of the Spirit who makes us strong, loving, and wise.

We then address a fundamental question: "Who am I?" Claiming our identity as God's beloved sons created in the divine image, we consider what difference this makes in our lives. We look at gender as a social construct and what it means to "be a man." We claim that while males are born, men are made—that is, our social patterns more than our biological sex shape various expressions of masculinity.

Next, we look at values and how they shape our lives. We examine how the "Man Box" of certain values affects us. We ask you to consider your "preferred self" to name values most important to you in forming your life. We then look at disciplines, or practices, to nurture our inner life for loving God, others, and ourselves. Ranging from meditating on scripture or other formative texts to walking in the woods, these practices help us experience a life of freedom, love, and peace that God offers us.

We then look at how we're created to live in community. This is the place we are welcomed as we are and find belonging. In community, we move beyond isolation and shame to a nurturing environment for our healing and growth. From here, we consider the gifts of friendships that invite us from rugged individualism to open connections with others for more meaningful and deeper relationships.

Finally, we examine our purpose and service in life. We state that our purpose is to enjoy and extend God's abundant life of freedom, love, and peace. As we follow Jesus and align our lives with God's purpose, we play our part to establish God's shalom in the world. This is our service. How this is played out varies from person to person. We close this section with a brief look at some roles we play in life. These are examined in more depth in the final section of this book.

We also offer extra materials and exercises in the resources section at the back of the book and at bit.ly/LivingThatMatters.

EXPERIENCES

Steve

Who we are is largely shaped by our experiences.

Through our experiences, we learn to trust and mistrust, connect and isolate, build self-esteem and pile up shame, and discover meaning and purpose. Our life experiences also have a lot to do with the kind of relationship we have with God.

We are formed by all sorts of things:

- Relationships with our parents and siblings
- Friendships in our community and school
- Intimate and broken relationships
- Struggles to discover our identity
- Explorations of our sexuality
- Opportunities to pursue, and denials of, our interests
- Failures and accomplishments
- Emotional, physical, or sexual abuse
- Neglect or lack of affirmation and love
- Bullying, discrimination, or racism
- Being let down or held up by others
- Support and guidance from significant adults
- Activities in school, athletics, and the arts
- Involvement in church or a faith community
- Encounters and disillusionment with God
- Relational, spiritual, and vocational crises

Love and suffering form us the most.

Experiences of love are powerful; they shape our lives in positive ways. We do well to claim these blessings with gratitude.

Experiences of suffering can misshape our lives and leave us wounded and broken. Difficult as they are, we can claim these experiences as times for growth.[2] As ecumenical teacher Richard Rohr puts it, our primary teachers are brokenness, failure, death, and woundedness—not ideas or doctrines. God can use suffering as well as love to transform our lives.[3]

For example, I was bullied in school. My mother taught me, "Sticks and stones may hurt my bones, but words will never hurt me." This wasn't true for me. Painful experiences of physical and emotional bullying sank deep into me.

Emotional wounds were far more hurtful and lasting than my broken nose from being kicked in the face.

Later, when I became an adult, God used these experiences to help me relate with youth in our Peacemakers program. I could encourage students to transform conflict and violence in their lives because I knew firsthand about such difficult experiences. As my spiritual director used to tell me, in the economy of God's grace, nothing is wasted, for God can use all our experiences for something good.

🗨 FOR CONVERSATION

Use these questions as part of the sharing life stories exercise (see pp. 28) to help groups connect at a deeper level.

1. Of your life experiences, which have been especially formative for you?
2. What are you most grateful for?
3. What good has come from your difficult experiences? How has God used them to shape your life?

EXERCISE: SHARING LIFE STORIES

This is a good exercise for new groups just beginning or for existing groups who want to relate at a deeper level.

Reflecting on our life experiences can open our eyes to see how we have been formed. This can help us grow in understanding both ourselves and others. It can also help us become more aware of how God has been active in our lives.

If you're using this handbook as a group, consider sharing your life experiences through storytelling. Not many men have had the chance to tell their life story. It's a powerful way to get to know one another at a deeper level than men usually relate to others.

- Allow each member to tell their story, one person at each gathering.
- Determine how long your gatherings will be (for example, 90 minutes is common).
- Agree as a group how much time to allow for individual storytelling and how much for group responses and questions.
- As you prepare your story before the meeting, consider the list of experiences at the beginning of this topic and the "For Conversation" questions listed on page 31.

Listen and respond to everyone's story before moving on in this handbook.

GOD

Steve

One of the oldest descriptions of the divine states that God is "merciful and gracious, slow to anger, and abounding in steadfast love and faithfulness" (Exodus 34:6). Jesus reveals in the flesh God's loving nature.

And John, Jesus' most intimate companion, proclaims that God is love and loves the whole world (John 3:16). He then invites us to love in response to God's love for us (1 John 4:16–21).

The first article in the Mennonite confession of faith claims that life is all about God's love in its variety of expressions:

> God's awesome glory and enduring compassion are perfect in holy love. God's sovereign power and unending mercy are perfect in almighty love. God's knowledge of all things and care for creation are perfect in preserving love. God's abounding grace and wrath against sinfulness are perfect in righteous love. God's readiness to forgive and power to transform are perfect in redemptive love. God's unlimited justice and continuing patience with humankind are perfect in suffering love. God's infinite freedom and constant self-giving are perfect in faithful love.[4]

Divine love is unconditional and universal. God's boundless love reaches around the world to all people of all faiths and throughout the universe for all eternity. As all people are created in God's image, all are also God's beloved children, regardless of culture, creed, or deed.

The Bible presents a variety of images for God. While most are masculine, others are feminine, illustrating that God is neither male nor female but transcends gender. For example, Sophia (translated as Wisdom) in the Hebrew Bible represents the divine feminine and is the source of our wisdom.[5]

Of the many images and metaphors for God, the most important, perhaps, is God as a loving parent. Isaiah says God is like a mother with compassionate love for the child of her womb (49:14–16). Hosea speaks of God as being like a parent with a fierce love for wayward children (11:1–9). And Jesus likens God to a compassionate, forgiving father who restores his lost son to life (Luke 15:11–32).

In *The Return of the Prodigal Son*, Henri Nouwen writes, "More than any other story in the Gospels, the parable of the prodigal son expresses the boundlessness of God's compassionate love."[6] When Nouwen first saw Rembrandt's painting

The Return of the Prodigal Son (see the painting in "Images of God" at bit.ly/ LivingThatMatters), the image of God's loving embrace prompted him to write:

> My heart leapt.... The tender embrace of father and son expressed everything I desired. I was, indeed, the son exhausted from long travels; I wanted to be embraced; I was looking for a home where I could feel safe. The son-come-home was all I was and all that I wanted to be.... I desired only to rest safely in a place ... where I could feel at home.[7]

What we believe about God matters because our faith forms us. Pastor and writer A. W. Tozer said, "We tend by a secret law of the soul to move toward our mental image of God. This is true not only of the individual Christian, but of the church."[8] How we see God affects who we become and what we witness. For example, those who see God as a demanding judge tend to be more judgmental, whereas those who see God as a loving parent tend to be more loving.

Pointing to the need for healing our image of God, priest Brennan Manning asserts: "So many of us have images of God that fill us with fear, anxiety, and apprehension. It is true that we make our images of God. It is even truer that our images of God make us." As a recovering alcoholic who experienced God's love, Manning shared:

> When I am really in conscious communion with the reality of the wild, passionate, relentless, stubborn, pursuing, tender love of God in Jesus Christ for me, then it's not that I have to or I got to or I must or I should or I ought; suddenly, I want to change because I know how deeply I'm loved.
>
> One of the wonderful results of my consciousness of God's staggering love for me as I am is the freedom not to be who I should be or who others want me to be. I can be who I really am.[9]

Experiencing God's love restored Manning from his destructive addiction and led him to freedom as a beloved son. In his renewed life, he embodied God's tender, compassionate love among many broken people suffering in addiction. His image and experience of God formed him into a loving person who could enjoy and extend God's abundant life.

> For an exercise, see **"Images of God"** and consider **"God's Love, Judgment, and Salvation"** at bit.ly/LivingThatMatters.

 **FOR CONVERSATION**

1. Who or what is God to you?
2. How has your view of God changed during your life's journey?
3. How have men in the history of patriarchy created God in their own "image" or as an authoritarian figure to serve their own interests?

JESUS

Steve

One of the great mysteries of our faith is that God was revealed in Jesus of Nazareth. "He is the image of the invisible God" (Colossians 1:15). Jesus reveals in the flesh what God is like, the way of love, and how to be fully human.

The Mennonite confession of faith states:

> We humbly recognize that God far surpasses human comprehension and understanding. We also gratefully acknowledge that God has spoken to humanity and related to us in many and various ways. We believe that God has spoken above all in the only Son, the Word who became flesh and revealed the divine being and character.[10]

God is active among all people of various faiths and is most fully revealed in Jesus the Christ—God's anointed one.

He was Jesus and he is the Christ—a human person who lived on the earth and a universal presence seeking to unite everyone and everything for one new humanity for God's peace (Galatians 3:28; Ephesians 2:14–15). As we sing in one hymn: "In Christ there is no east or west, in him no south or north, / but one great fellowship of love throughout the whole wide earth."[11]

By looking at what Jesus revealed, we know that God, who is love, intends us to have abundant life and to establish shalom. In the Gospels, we see Jesus

- embodying compassion,
- teaching the ways of God,
- healing brokenness,
- confronting evil and wrong,
- relating to the marginalized,
- crossing social divides,
- embracing all with love,
- seeking peace with justice.

Jesus is the archetypal human. In other words, he teaches and models how to be a whole human being as God intends. Thomas Yoder Neufeld writes in *Peaceful at Heart*:

> To insist that Jesus is the template for what it means to be a man is not to ask for slavish imitation of a first-century Galilean wandering teacher, healer and

exorcist. But seeing Jesus as model does mean loving God and others, including enemies, like he did; caring for others, rich and poor alike, like he did; being hungry for justice, like he was; loving and making peace, like he did; serving others, like he did; being truthful, like he was; taking up the cross, as he did; trusting God with one's life, like he did. In short, it means learning from him to be "perfect."[12]

Because of the resurrection of Jesus and the universal presence of Christ, we are confident in his transforming power in our lives. Richard Rohr writes:

Jesus comes forth from [God] into the world to say, "This is what God is doing. Look at me. I'm what God is doing. And I'm the whole process, from beginning to end." . . . Because of Jesus' life, death, and resurrection, we know ahead of time that the final chapter is always resurrection. Though so much of life is filled with suffering, disappointment, disillusionment, absurdity, and dying, God will turn all our crucifixions into resurrections. Look at it in Jesus, believe it in Jesus, . . . love it in Jesus, and let it take shape in your own soul.[13]

FOR CONVERSATION

1. In what ways does Jesus' radical life speak to men in our culture today?
2. If you identify as a follower of Jesus,
   a. How has following Jesus formed your life?
   b. What about following Jesus is life-giving for you?
   c. What about following Jesus is difficult for you?

If you don't identify as a follower of Jesus,
   a. In what ways might following Jesus be life-giving for you?
   b. In what ways might following Jesus be difficult for you?

SPIRIT

Steve

Jesus did not leave his followers but continues to be present with us in the Spirit. This is another great mystery—that God, Jesus, and the Spirit are present and active in our lives, forming what we are becoming as whole human beings in God's image.

The Mennonite confession of faith states that

> the Spirit of God is God's presence and power active in the world. The Spirit, or breath, of God acted in creation and continues to act in the creative process throughout the world, in expected and unexpected places. God's Spirit was a source of power and revealed God's wisdom to prophets and other holy people. By the power of the Spirit, Jesus healed the sick, cast out unclean spirits, and proclaimed the reign of God. By the same Spirit, he offered his life to God and was raised from the dead.[14]

The same Spirit that was at work from creation, in Jesus, and among God's people is active in our lives today. This same Spirit is also present among people of various faith traditions. While other religious traditions may not recognize Jesus in the way we do, the Spirit may be acknowledged as a universal Presence. As Choctaw elder and Christian leader Steven Charleston states, Spirit is a "marker—a placeholder—for the conscious, spiritual presence many people from different religious traditions would call God, or Creator."[15]

Recognizing this helps us appreciate the universal work of the Spirit outside our faith tradition.

As God's transforming presence and power, the Spirit

- brings things into being—creating out of chaos, breathing life into things, restoring life from death (Genesis 1:2; 2:7; Ezekiel 37:1–10);
- unites diverse people groups—reconciling those of different cultures, classes, and creeds (Acts 2:1–11; Ephesians 4:1–6);
- guides our discernment—revealing new directions as God's way of love is discerned in community (John 16:12–13; Acts 15:1–29; 1 Corinthians 14:7–31);
- develops gifts for service—granting us abilities for the common good (1 Corinthians 12:1–11; Ephesians 4:11–12);

- empowers us for action—making us bold and confident in the face of difficulty (Acts 1:8; 3:1–4:31; 6:8–8:1);
- forms our character—developing fruits of the Spirit and making us strong, loving, and wise as we are formed into God's image (Galatians 5:22–23; 2 Timothy 1:7; 2 Corinthians 3:18).

The song "New Earth, Heavens New," found in Anabaptist hymnals, expresses that the Spirit is moving in our lives and world, reshaping humankind, the earth, and heavens.[16]

Let the Spirit form us into "new men" for a newly formed earth.

FOR CONVERSATION

1. What new things of the Spirit have you witnessed?
2. What is the Spirit shaping in your life?
3. What fruits is the Spirit forming in your character?
4. In what ways do you see the Spirit creating "new men" in the image of God for society today?

IDENTITY

Steve

When Jesus was baptized, a voice from heaven said, "You are my beloved Son; with you I am well pleased" (Luke 3:22 NABRE). Can we claim this truth for ourselves—that we are beloved sons of God? Yes, we can. We read that human beings are created in the image of God (Genesis 1:26–27; 9:5–6; James 3:9) and that we are children of God (Galatians 3:26; Romans 8:16; 1 John 3:1–2).

Anabaptist thinker Noel Moules writes:

> When I ask, "Who am I?" from the perspective of Jesus, I am told, "You are made in the 'image and likeness of God.' . . . We have been shaped from the earth, yet brought alive by the very Spirit-breath of God; quite literally a mixture of heaven and earth—completely one with wild nature, yet sharing personhood with God. This is something dynamic, not static; calling each of us to be the image of God in the way we live. Jesus is our reference point. In him we see the image and likeness of God most clearly revealed. Jesus says what is true for him can be true for us also.
>
> This is my fingerprint.
>
> What is true for me is true for everyone. God's image and likeness is seen most fully in the diversity of humanity together. This reality has revolutionised my life. Previously most people were peripheral to my vision. . . . Then suddenly everyone I met began to look different. . . . The image of God in them began to appear before my eyes.[17]

Because all people are created in God's image, all are God's beloved children regardless of culture, creed, or deed. This truth influences how we look at and relate to others and is the basis for living in love and peace. Peace activist John Dear writes:

> Practicing nonviolence means claiming our fundamental identity as beloved sons and daughters of the God of peace, and thus, going forth into the world as peacemakers to love every other human being. . . .
>
> The problem is: we don't know who we are. . . . The challenge then is to remember who we are, and therefore be nonviolent to ourselves and others.[18]

In a peace education program that I led in the Peacemakers Academy, in public schools, and in a psychiatric hospital, every class opened with, "Who are you?" Participants responded, "A precious person who deserves respect." I explained that because we are created in the divine image, (1) all people are precious and deserve respect, and (2) this is the foundation for making peace with others and ourselves.

Claiming for ourselves who we are as God's beloved sons can be difficult. This is especially true when we fall or fail, leaving us feeling shame with a low sense of self. For these moments, I offer men in our retreats a saying of Richard Rohr: "We are beloved sons of God who sh*t." This statement makes an important separation between who we are and what we do. Yes, we sin, but that doesn't change who we are.[19]

In *The Inner Voice of Love*, Henri Nouwen writes about discovering who he was in a crisis:

[When you] go deeper into your heart and thus deeper into the heart of God . . . you become what you already are—a child of God; it lets you embody more and more the truth of your being; it makes you claim the God within you. You are tempted to think that you are a nobody. . . . But this is a mistake. You must trust the depth of God's presence in you and live from there.[20]

Elsewhere Nouwen writes,

From the moment we claim the truth of being the Beloved, we are faced with the call to become who we are. Becoming the Beloved is the great spiritual journey we have to make.[21]

Imagine what the world would be like if we all remembered who we are as God's beloved children and if we related as siblings of one human family.

🗣 FOR CONVERSATION

1. What difference might it make in your life to really believe and live as a beloved child of God?
2. How does Rohr's saying "We are beloved sons of God who sh*t" speak to you?
3. When do you recognize the image of God in yourself or others?
4. When is it difficult for you to recognize your identity, or that of others, as a child of God?

GENERO

Steve

Many men have heard the expression "Be a man." But what does this mean? What makes someone a man?

In American culture we have too often heard the same message that sank deep into Joe Ehrmann, coach and former NFL football player—"Be a man." Ehrmann learned from his father and on the field that "men don't need. Men don't want. Men don't touch. Men don't feel. If you're going to be a man in this world, you better learn how to dominate and control people and circumstances." Now a pastor and an activist-educator, Ehrmann teaches males other ways of being men.[22]

In talking about being men, it's important to understand the differences between sex, gender, and masculinity. While these concepts are complex (as will also be seen later when we discuss sexual identity), generally speaking, here's what we mean by these words:

- *Sex:* The biological classification of a person based on male and female sexual organs.
- *Gender:* Social characteristics of a person based on cultural expressions of females and males and how individuals understand their identity.[23]
- *Masculinity:* Socially constructed traits, behaviors, and roles associated with boys and men.

We are born with certain sexual organs that classify us as male, female, or intersex (with both male and female or ambiguous sexual anatomy). While our sex is usually fixed or assigned at birth, our gender is more fluid and is largely shaped by our culture. In other words, while males are born, men are made. We are socially constructed. Social learning more than male bodies determines masculinity.

We refer to this process as the social construction of gender. How men act and what roles they play are influenced by what is taught and caught in their culture—that is, the beliefs, values, attitudes, and roles of their society.[24] These are not fixed but vary from culture to culture. As R. W. Connell shows in her work *Masculinities*, there is not one masculinity; rather, there are many masculinities. There is no set, natural masculinity with clear differences between what's masculine and what's feminine. Connell illustrates this with very different, and sometimes opposite, ways of being men and women across cultures.[25] Our book *Peaceful at Heart* illustrates that multiple masculinities exist even among Anabaptist men.

Jamie Pitts discusses gender construction in *Peaceful at Heart*. He writes that the process of gender formation offers good news:

> If gender is complex, dynamic, and culturally specific, then ancient patterns of organizing society and defining individuals along gendered lines may be open to change. For example, the common equation of men with domination and violence need not be the last word. Mennonite and other men can explore what it means to be men who are peaceful at heart.[26]

Against the prevailing model of being a man in his patriarchal culture, Jesus modeled an alternative masculinity. We see Jesus

- feeling compassion,
- expressing tenderness,
- confronting wrongs,
- crying in grief,
- touching people,
- respecting women,
- having close friends,
- resisting the use of force,
- being willing to suffer rather than retaliate,
- serving rather than dominating.

To explore the differences between healthy and conventional masculinity as a group, consider the **"Reconstructing Masculinities"** exercise in the resources section at the back of the book. This exercise exposes the limiting and toxic expressions of dominant masculinity in culture and invites us out of the "Man Box" and into the circle of good men. [27]

In these ways, Jesus models a healthy masculinity.

Today, dominant forms of masculinity persist that not only feed into the abuse, oppression, and violation of vulnerable persons but also negatively affect males.[28] As men following Jesus, we want to embody and promote healthy masculinity for the good of all around us.

FOR CONVERSATION

1. When you were a child, what was taught or caught about what it means to be a man?
2. If you were another gender, how would your life be different?
3. How have you struggled with or resisted masculine stereotypes in our culture?
4. Who or what has helped you most in becoming a man?
5. What kind of man do you desire to be?

PURPOSE

Steve

Why do we exist? We have a purpose in life linked to God's great project. Once we discover this, we realize our lives matter and that we are part of something bigger than ourselves. Knowing and serving this purpose gives our life focus, meaning, and joy.

Our purpose is linked with God's purpose to establish shalom in the world. *Shalom* is the rich Hebrew word for a peaceable order with collective abundance, security, and justice throughout all creation. It's the universal wholeness God seeks to restore on earth.[29]

Jesus knew and served his own purpose. He sums it up in these words: "I came that they may have life and have it abundantly" (John 10:10). John describes God's abundant life that Jesus brought in terms of freedom, love, and peace. In the last recorded conversations Jesus has with his friends, he says that he wants them to enjoy and extend this life (John 15:1–16; 20:21).

In short, this is also our purpose—to enjoy and extend God's abundant life.

Enlarging this in terms of John's gospel, our purpose in life is to enjoy and extend God's abundant life of freedom, love, and peace (outlined in the table[30]).

Enjoy and	God wants all people to enjoy a good life together. Life's a gift in which to delight and find great joy.[a]
Extend	God calls us to extend this life. We are not to enjoy this life alone but to share it with others.[b]
God's	All this is from God, the creator of life and love. God's purpose is revealed in Jesus.[c] And God's presence in the Spirit empowers us to serve our purpose.
Abundant life	God intends life with material, spiritual, and social abundance. Witness the garden of Eden, fruitful fields, feasts of food and wine, and the city of heaven.[d]
Of freedom,	It involves freedom from bondage and freedom for abundant life. We are to be free from oppression, sins, and brokenness to enjoy God's good life.[e]
Love, and	The heart of this life is love. God is love and desires that we live in love with God, self, and all people, sharing of ourselves and our resources.[f]
Peace.	The fruit of all of this is peace, or God's shalom—a peaceable order with collective abundance, security, and justice throughout all of creation.[g]

We all have a common purpose in life. How we serve this varies from person to person. We each have a personal mission in God's project. In the Bible, we see a whole cast of characters, each playing their part in serving their mission.

Consider the particular mission of a few of God's people:

- Moses—to free the Hebrews
- Esther—to save the Jews
- Nehemiah—to rebuild the walls of Jerusalem
- Jeremiah—to restore hope among the exiles
- Mary—to bear Jesus into the world
- Luke—to tell the story of Jesus and the church
- Paul—to share the gospel to Gentiles

These people played prominent roles serving their purpose in life. But most characters in God's story are never named. If they are, they receive only honorable mention. Like Joseph—the carpenter and husband of Mary—who simply did what God asked of him. Over forty people are named in the genealogy of Jesus. Some are well known, others not. Some are virtuous, others not. Most of us fall in the "others" category. Nevertheless, we too, in the legacy of Jesus, have a part to play in serving our purpose.

> To reflect on and identify your purpose in life, consider the exercise **"Discerning My Personal Mission"** in the resources section.

FOR CONVERSATION

1. Do you have a sense of purpose or mission in life? If so, how would you describe it? (You may want to discuss what you found in the personal mission exercise in the resources section.)
2. How are you serving your purpose?
3. What direction, meaning, and joy has this given you? What frustrations or difficulties have you faced?
4. How has this purpose shaped your life?
5. How does this purpose vary from what's often expected of men in our culture?

VALUES

Don

Paul writes in Philippians 4:8–9 (NRSVA):

> Finally, beloved, whatever is true, whatever is honourable, whatever is just, whatever is pure, whatever is pleasing, whatever is commendable, if there is any excellence and if there is anything worthy of praise, think about these things. Keep on doing the things that you have learned and received and heard and seen in me, and the God of peace will be with you.

Our values define us. We live them, whether we are aware of them or not. When we are young and less mature, we take on the values we learn from others around us. As we become adults, it's vitally important that we make our own decisions about who we want to be in this world.

We pick up our values from various places. If we think of ourselves as a tree, our family and community are like the roots that get us started in the world. The values we receive from them tend to be long-lasting. Faith communities can also greatly influence our values. The importance of these values is often impressed upon us with an authority that makes them central in our lives. Our personal faith journeys in relationship with God, and our study of scripture or other resources for inner growth, also inform our values.

In today's world, we are bombarded with messages about what it means to be a man. As technology—especially social media—connects us to the entire world, it's almost like we're embedded in a nonstop movie of masculine images and values. Patriarchal norms, sometimes called the "Man Box," dominate that movie. For centuries, these traditionally accepted definitions of what it means to be a man have determined the behavior of most men.[31]

But as the saying goes, times are a-changin'. In recent years, we've witnessed a strong challenge to the traditional values of patriarchy. Many people are saying it's time to paint a different picture of what it means to be a man.

As men in today's rapidly changing social environment, what values will we choose? It's up to us to take inventory of our values and make choices about who we will be and how we will live. As maturing adults, we have the opportunity to act intentionally and in an informed way.

Making these decisions about our values is one of our most critical tasks as human beings and as communities.

As a therapist, I often talk about the "preferred self" as a way to encourage clients to become conscious of their personal values. Who do they want to be in this world? What values do they want to show in their relationships with others? If they are parents, what values do they want to model for their children?

Many people live with their "heads in the sand"; they've never thought about who they really want to be. This was true for one man I talked with, whose behavior had hurt others greatly and almost destroyed one of his cherished relationships. When I asked him what his preferred self looked like and what values he longed to live, he stopped cold. He realized he had never considered such a question. He had always acted just from his impulses in the moment. How unfortunate for him and the people he loved!

Unlike some of our human impulses, God's will for us is always good. It's recorded for us in the Bible (Colossians 1:15; Hebrews 1:1–3) and shown in the life of Jesus. As Christians, we believe our creator God calls us to live beyond our impulses and learn to open ourselves to God's goodness in our lives.

As men, we have the opportunity—and also the responsibility—to pull our heads out of the sand and make some intentional decisions about who we want to be. Jesus' way of life is freeing and life-giving, and he calls us to live according to the same values he did—by that which is true, honorable, just, pure, commendable, and excellent, ultimately pleasing to God and to God's creation.

FOR CONVERSATION

1. What have been the biggest influences on the values you hold?
2. How would you describe your own experience of the "Man Box" (traditional patriarchy)?
3. What values within traditional patriarchy do you find helpful? What values do you reject?
4. In what ways are your values the same or different from the society around you?
5. What values (and corresponding practices) would you like to live out as your "preferred self"?

PRACTICES

Steve

To his friends and followers, Jesus says, "Abide in me as I abide in you" (see John 15:1–11). This invites us to an inner connection with Christ—our source of spiritual vitality, growth, and fruitfulness. In Greek, the word Jesus uses for "abide" stirs the imagination. It's *meno*, which means to abide, dwell, or make our home in him. *Meno*, as Jesus uses it elsewhere, refers to both the inner and outer ways of following Jesus. In other words, abiding in Jesus affects our inner connection to God and our outer conduct, our receiving and our extending of Christ's love.[32]

As Jesus showed us, spiritual practices are about making space for God and paying attention to God's presence and call in our lives. They nurture the goals of our spiritual life—loving God, ourselves, and others.

The Anabaptist-Mennonite tradition emphasizes following Jesus in his way of love, justice, and peace. To help heal social problems such as sexism, racism, and violence, we need spiritual practices that guide us in becoming like Jesus by "dwelling" in him. These practices will form qualities in us such as compassion, courage, and sacrifice. Christian peacemakers like Dorothy Day, Martin Luther King Jr., and Oscar Romero are examples of people who rigorously engaged in both prayer and action.

There are many ways to be attentive to God in our life. Here are a few examples:

- Prayer—being with God in thought, word, or silence
- Devotional reading—focusing on scripture or spiritual reading
- Bible study—learning by careful study of scripture
- *Lectio divina*—using an ancient method to pray with the scriptures
- Meditation—reflecting on a verse, phrase or image, or something in creation
- Contemplation—resting with God in inner silence
- Faith imagination—imagining Jesus with you and noticing what he does and says
- Fasting—giving up something to be present to another thing
- Retreat—creating extended time away to pay attention to God
- Journaling—reflecting in the form of writing
- Spiritual friendship—focusing on spiritual life with a companion (see "Spiritual Friendships" in the resources section)
- Spiritual direction—receiving support and guidance from a spiritual mentor

While scripture has long been a source of spiritual inspiration, people have also found nature, art, music, icons, labyrinths, and other means as sources for experiencing God. We can sit still for some practices and walk for others. We can do these in solitude or with other spiritual companions. Praying with an open Bible in silence is simply one of many practices.

Take nature, for example. Long before written scripture, there was creation—God's first Word. And long before tabernacles, temples, and churches, there was nature—God's great outdoor sanctuary. Many people report feeling close to God in nature. This was true of Jesus, like prophets before him, who retreated into the wilderness to commune with God. Hans Denck, an early Anabaptist mystic, believed that God is in all things and "speaks clearly in everyone, in the deaf... and blind, even... in beasts, even in leaves and grass, stone and wood, heaven and earth, and all that is in them, that they may hear and do his will."[33]

I realize this as I walk in wild spaces or sit in my deer stand. When I simply sit quietly in a tree, I'm present to life in the natural world around me. As I am still and attentive, I feel at one with the world and notice things I usually wouldn't see. At Pathways Retreat, where I live, a group meets in the woods every Friday for a spiritual practice. Participants come with the intention of looking and listening for God and reflecting on their experience.

We are free to find our own unique way to pay attention to God in our lives. My first spiritual director offers this invitation to all of us: Pray as you can, not as you think you should, and allow the Spirit to work in you.

> For more on spiritual practices, see **"Resources for Spiritual Growth"** at bit.ly/LivingThatMatters.

FOR CONVERSATION

1. How are you tending your inner life?
2. Of the many spiritual practices listed here (or others), which have you found helpful?
3. Recalling what Jesus says in John 15:1–11 about abiding in him and bearing fruit, what practices are especially fruitful for you? What fruit are they bearing?

COMMUNITY

Don

Unless we live alone on a deserted island, we interact with others. This means we all live in community. How we each experience life in community varies widely, however. And how each of us feels about being alone or being in relationship with others changes with the community experiences that collect in us over time.

Historically, humans gathered in relatively small, tight-knit groupings based on family ties, geography, common experiences, culture, and religion. Shared experiences and values strengthened the connections within each group. They also created clear distinctions between "us" and "them."

Such group distinctions are not so clear today. Configurations of family, culture, and religion are changing rapidly. Given how mobile society is, even geography is much less a factor now in defining groups. All of this means that our circles of connections are generally much broader and more diverse than in the past. In some ways, our circles of connection are also less reliable than in previous generations.

Community is the ground in which our lives are formed. Our community might be primarily family—maybe even only our nuclear family—or it might be a diverse group of people with whom we interact.

The power of example in community is significant. In many ways, others' actions have greater influence in our lives than their words. And this influence can be good or not so good for our development.

As we grow from children into adults, we interact with our environment, including other human beings. We listen and watch, absorbing what the community around us models. Generally, though not always, we identify most closely with our same-sex or same-gender community members. As boys, we tend to identify with our fathers, brothers, uncles, grandfathers, male neighbors, or other male members of our faith or cultural community.

In this male world, basic skills of emotional intelligence tend to be devalued and thus not taught. To use just one image, this leaves many boys and men feeling as if they are navigating a maze blindfolded. Healthy relationships are difficult when we haven't been taught how to relate, especially since true relationships must be built through vulnerability and empathy.

Boys and men who show emotion, other than anger, often get made fun of. This drives our natural relational selves underground, and we end up isolated and lonely. Men relate to other men while doing activities together such as work or sport but seldom experience deeper connections with other men. Messages to boys and men often include valuing independence and isolation and devaluing interpersonal skills that support healthy relationships with others.

Jesus, during his time of ministry on earth, deliberately surrounded himself with community. He chose twelve men to be his closest companions, and he interacted regularly with other people around him. Although he interacted in provocative and strong ways with some of these people, such as the religious leaders (see Matthew 12:34), his overall message focused on reconciling broken relationships, both with God and with each other (John 13:34–35).

Ultimately, Jesus chooses to call us friends (John 15:15). What a wonderful image of God's invitation to us to gather as God's children in community.

Personally, I have greatly valued my experiences with my faith community—both locally and in the broader interfaith world in various places I've lived and worked. I've been particularly fortunate to participate in the larger Mennonite community through involvement in Mennonite education settings and conference gatherings. The sense of belonging and the group experiences of worship during those years have formed me and been incredibly life-giving. I live in gratefulness for these opportunities in my life!

Community at its best is a place of welcome where people can find unconditional love and support while also receiving encouragement and guidance toward healthy living.

For men, the opportunity to move beyond isolation and shame comes through an invitation to belong at a deep level, to experience safety in vulnerability, and to be able to be fully ourselves and even own our regrettable behaviors. It's an opportunity to be surrounded by true friendship. This kind of nurturing environment can help heal and grow us so that we can have healthier intimate relationships and find belonging and peace in our lives.

FOR CONVERSATION

1. How have you been formed by community?
2. When are you more comfortable interacting with others, and when do you prefer to be alone?
3. What do you value most about the interactions you have with others?
4. What benefits or limitations of community have you experienced?

FRIENDSHIP

Don

The image of the solitary cowboy riding off into the rugged West has long inspired boys and men to follow the call to independence, conquest, and heroism. Unfortunately, it also represents deep themes of isolation and loneliness that many men experience.

More often than not, with inadequate lessons and role models for healthy relationships, we find ourselves surrounded by people but longing to be fully known and loved by others despite our own inadequacies. We often end up hurting the people closest to us while trying desperately to gain their love.

Is this just how men are? Are we simply less relationally wired, and does that mean we can rely less on others for our well-being? Images and messages that dominate male socialization tell us this is true. But experts suggest it's not. Family therapist Terry Real says that boys are "systematically pushed away from the full exercise of emotional expressiveness and the skills for making and appreciating deep connection" and that "the wounded boy grows up to become a wounding man, inflicting upon those closest to him the very distress he refuses to acknowledge within himself."[34]

Many men have extensive connections with other men—through work, sports (as participants or fans), and shared interests and pursuits. But the truth is that for far too many men these connections are shallow and not welcoming of true sharing of self, especially when the presence of challenges and struggles would require deep vulnerability. Fears, too, of being identified in any way with questionable sexual intentions, either for other men or for women who do not welcome such interest, creates much anxiety in us as we tune in to our longings for connection and our awareness of lacking something. For some of us, true experience of friendship is fleeting. For too many of us, loneliness and isolation are the sentence for living up to today's expectations of masculinity.

The intense 1978 epic war drama *The Deer Hunter* touched me deeply when I first viewed it in the mid-1980s. In the movie, a group of friends find their friendships tested and torn as they move from a small steel town in Pennsylvania to the treacherous theater of the Vietnam War. Experiencing this portrayal of male relationships affected me profoundly. At the time, I was coming out of an intensely meaningful period of friendships in the early '80s during my high school years—friendships that remain deeply important for me today. In many ways, *The Deer Hunter* set the stage for my empathy for the difficult lives that men face.

The neglect of, and sometimes outright attack on, boys' and men's natural relational selves leaves men, and our world, impoverished. For those who live with and love boys and men, navigating the murky and sometimes dangerous waters of relating with them demands patience and perseverance. It also—very importantly—requires strong boundaries when a male's best intentions sour into hostility and even aggression. Men need to recognize, own, and seek a way to heal impulses to defend ourselves and hurt others. These impulses may often actually be cries for connection and closeness that we desperately crave even while they seem out of reach.

Christians have the benefit of a faith that is relationally based. Jesus showed the importance of friendship. Reaching out to all of us, Jesus says, "No longer do I call you servants, for the servant does not know what his master is doing; but I have called you friends, for all that I have heard from my Father I have made known to you" (John 15:15 ESV).

To all men I say, *longing for and seeking true friendship is right and life-giving.* Becoming honest and open to others so we can develop meaningful friendships is a vulnerable practice. We will not always be comfortable doing this. But we are created as relational human beings, and we all—individually and as a society— are strengthened and enriched by connecting our lives in meaningful ways with others.

FOR CONVERSATION

1. What is your experience and understanding of differences between men's and women's needs for relationships? In what ways might these differences not be so different?

2. What do you risk by becoming more open and vulnerable with others?

3. What might make it easier for you to pursue meaningful connections with others?

SERVICE

Steve

Our purpose in life is to enjoy and extend God's abundant life of freedom, love, and peace. As we follow Jesus and align our lives with God's purpose, we play our part in establishing God's shalom in the world. This is our service.

Paul writes, "For we are what [God] has made us, created in Christ Jesus for good works, which God prepared beforehand so that we may walk in them" (Ephesians 2:10). How we serve and what good works we do varies from person to person according to our different gifts, calls, and situations in life. And we can serve any place we find ourselves.

God's Spirit works through us to do good things, great and small. Most of our service happens in what appear to be smaller things. But Jesus points out that what may seem small is truly significant—like giving someone food or clothing, welcoming a stranger, caring for the sick, and visiting the imprisoned (Matthew 25:34–36).

Consider parts that men play and their roles in the biblical story (see table).

Steward	Tend the earth as a keeper of God's creation
Warrior	Serve and protect all people and the earth
Lover	Delight in what is lovely and beautiful
Partner	Live with a companion in a committed relationship
Father	Provide for, nurture, love, and bless one's family
Mentor	Guide others along their journey as they mature
Healer	Restore health and wholeness through acts of care
Prophet	Address issues with God's word and will
Leader	Influence and empower others
Elder	Embody and extend wisdom

Jesus played these parts as he served God's mission of establishing shalom. Each of us has one or more of these parts within us that can be expressed in many ways through our service.

These parts have both inner and outer aspects:

Inner dimensions and dynamics. Some call these archetypes—interior imprints or images deep within us. These energetic parts enliven our service.[35]

From a psychological perspective, they are inherited from generations of human experience. From a faith perspective, we add that these are imprints of God's Spirit working within us, empowering our service.

Outer aspects. Outer aspects of these parts are seen in how they are expressed in service. I have a friend, Wes, who models how these roles and his gifts and passions come together in a unique way. Wes is a master in martial arts in my Mennonite congregation. He didn't think he had gifts God could use until we started Peacemakers Academy, a Mennonite martial arts school. Wes came alive as he used his skills and followed his passion to work with youth to empower them to transform conflict and prevent violence. He didn't like his day job, but as a man on a mission exercising his gifts in service, he came alive with new life. His inner warrior and mentor energized him. As one observer remarked, "Who would have imagined that God would call a martial artist to help make peace!" Truly the Spirit works in wondrous ways, taking what we each offer for good in the world.

Along with others who are passionate about what they do, Wes could say, "I feed on this." God desires that we feed on our acts of service and the good we do—in other words, that our action is life-giving to us as well as others so that our service is sustainable. Jesus said to his followers, "My food is to do the will of [God] who sent me" (John 4:34).

> For a more complete description of the parts listed in this reflection, see **"Parts Men Play in Serving God's Shalom"** in the resources section.
>
> To consider your gifts and call, see the exercise **"Discerning Our Call to Service"** in the resources section.

 ## FOR CONVERSATION

1. How are you serving God's purpose in the world?
2. How does this feed or energize you?
3. Of the roles described in this reflection, which resonate with you?
4. What gifts do you have to offer in service? (You may want to discuss what you found in the "discerning our call" exercise.)
5. How do these perspectives compare with expectations our culture has of men regarding service?

As section 1 ends, let's stop to notice what's happening with us. After a minute of silence, discuss:

- How are we experiencing our open conversations?
- What gifts, difficulties, or tensions do we notice?
- Where is God's Spirit at work within and among us?

Human Needs

In This Section

Security

Action

Connectedness

Recognition

Meaning

INTRODUCTION

Don

I came that [you] may have life and have it abundantly.
—Jesus, John 10:10

OUR HUMAN EXPERIENCE shows us that not having our needs fulfilled can greatly decrease the quality of our lives. It can even mean the difference between life and death.

The difficulties we experience when our needs are not reasonably fulfilled can help us understand the often-tragic outcomes for human development and life on this planet. For instance, we can imagine what might happen when an infant, who is fully dependent on caregivers, does not receive proper care in one or more aspects of their life. Or when a nation violently invades a neighbor, taking by force what its members believe are limited resources needed for their own happiness.

From the earliest chapters of the Bible, the invitation of our creator God is to live in right relationship—with God, creation, each other, and ourselves. God created this world with rhythms and patterns that make it thrive. When this order is disturbed, natural consequences follow.

Jesus came down among us humans as God's Son to experience and model true humanity. My buddies and I used to sing a song in our youth that went: "This world is not my home, I'm just a passing through. My treasures are laid up, somewhere beyond the blue." Now that I've lived a few more years and journeyed alongside many fellow travelers, these lyrics feel shortsighted to me. They fail to encourage us to "seize the day," to take the opportunity to live fully today. They also allow us to ignore those for whom this journey on earth is heavy and long.

What are our needs as humans? Obviously, we have basic physical needs for nourishment and safety. These minimum requirements for biological survival are relatively easy to understand. When it comes to our other needs that help us become not only surviving but also thriving human beings, it's not so simple. Christians trying to live up to their understanding of the Bible's commands for selflessness and care for others (1 Corinthians 10:24; Philippians 2:4) have tended to dismiss these other, equally important, human needs. How these needs are met—or not—shapes our identity, who we become.

Coming to recognize and understand our legitimate identity needs is a key part of our life journey. It gives us the tools we need, as individuals and as a society, to live in ways that clear a more open path toward wholeness. Knowing our needs also helps us deal with experiences that could otherwise eat away at our well-being.

Men have traditionally been tasked with meeting many of the needs of their family, community, or nation through engaging in demanding and sometimes risky responsibilities such as hunting, fishing, exploring new lands for occupation, warring against neighboring communities over limited resources, or fending off intruders who threaten family or community. They become heroes when they succeed in these tasks and are shamed when they fall short.

Boys and men are often robbed of the ability to name and seek fulfillment of their own needs in healthy ways. This happens through society's failure to teach us the skills of self-reflection and emotional intelligence (how to understand and relate to our own emotions). It also happens through nonstop messages against any form of vulnerability or weakness.

To top it off, men often receive two primary messages that contradict each other: (1) be a self-sacrificing, disposable hero, and (2) claim your privileges as a male. These mixed messages can create deep confusion inside us, with tragic outcomes both personally and socially. Left without healthy means and hope, males too often make desperate attempts to meet their needs in ways that leave others used and broken.

We have the opportunity before us to begin building a much stronger, healthier understanding of our core identity needs and to nurture together a better outcome. In what follows, we will talk more about human identity needs, specifically in the lives of men. Using Vern Neufeld Redekop's human identity needs theory,[1] we will explore five core needs: (1) security, (2) action, (3) connectedness, (4) recognition, and (5) meaning.

Our hope is that greater understanding of how to fill our needs in a healthy way will result in better lives for men and for those who live with us and love us.

SECURITY

Don

Physical safety is a basic need that humans share with all creatures. Because our very existence depends on protection from external threats, we highly value and fiercely defend our security. So much so that a massive industry exists to support our personal and collective safety.

For men, the traditional role as protector of others who are more vulnerable has been a source of honor. This role of protector commonly takes place within a world of power and posturing that is traditionally ruled by men. How a man performs in this world often defines his masculinity. Men have taken the protector role so seriously that they've offered their very bodies—out of chivalrous concern for others, or to secure their own privilege and survival, or perhaps for recognition of their bravery and sacrifice. Millions of men have lost their lives as they've sought to protect others against threats in the natural environment or against human enemies on the battlefield. The hero-worship boys and men receive for such acts of bravery can be intoxicating.

Human security, though, is much broader than physical protection from injury and death. It also requires meeting physical needs for food, shelter, and clothing as well as emotional and psychological needs for security. Community, family, and individual well-being depend on respect for human rights—including rights to think independently, gather with others, and practice one's religion.

In earlier times, humans used to focus on basic survival needs. As expectations grew beyond the basics, we needed to think outside the box to provide for expanded ways of living. Men have taken their ideas to all corners of the globe, seeking to create conditions where their dependents can thrive. In a world of limited resources, however, security for one group has often meant scarcity for others. Men have traditionally been the ones expected to defend resources for their own group, even when it has meant maiming and killing outsiders. This role, repeated through thousands of generations of men, has molded a male identity that has made it seem normal for a male to use violent force. When encountering threats—real or imagined, individual or corporate—men are capable of terrible violence toward others.

Jesus' call to love our enemies (Matthew 5; Luke 6) and his modeling of self-sacrifice in the face of threat (Matthew 26; John 18) have challenged our reliance on violence. Conflicting understandings of how to maintain security have created an especially difficult dilemma for men in their role of maintaining security for others. Males within peace church groups have historically struggled with their identity as men, specifically because of feeling helpless as family members or neighbors have faced rape, pillage, and even death. Men who have taken the peace position in the face of threat have also had their masculinity called into question and been scorned by the larger community.

The need for security—physical or otherwise—highlights how fragile our human existence is and shows us the importance of turning to God's intentions for human well-being.

FOR CONVERSATION

1. What have been some of the greatest threats to your security?
2. When have you used violence to protect yourself or others? When have you refrained from using violence, and why?
3. How do you think Jesus' call to peacemaking applies to security?

ACTION

Don

In our society, we are often defined by our activities. Especially our work and play.

For many men, employment not only occupies a significant part of our daily life but also makes a statement about who we are. We are known by our occupation and respected for our ability to gain and hold a job so that we can support ourselves and the people dependent on us. Some men excel in this and find ways to contribute to their families and to the larger community. Others are worn down by unjust systems, poverty, and exclusion. Still others, because of various forms of disability, struggle to find meaningful employment and are unable to gain a sense of self-worth from their work.

Biblical references are readily available to support a focus on work and productivity. The book of Proverbs, for instance, contains a number of pithy statements about hard work. Take this one, for example: "The hand of the diligent will rule, while the lazy will be put to forced labor" (12:24).

Play is another major part of masculine identity formation. Men spend significant amounts of time and money chasing their idea of a good life. Many of these activities are life-giving for them, contributing to their health and personal development. Athletic activities, recreational pursuits, hobbies, and interests can all help boys and men express competitive drives and fulfill quests for excellence, accomplishment, companionship, and creativity. These activities can also provide entertainment for others.

Boys and men are also often oriented to doing and fixing. From early on, they receive messages and tasks that encourage developing skills and solving problems. In the context of helping others and sometimes at significant risk and self-sacrifice, boys and men often receive praise and honor for their achievements. These achievements are sometimes voluntary ("gentlemanly" deeds of sacrifice) and other times a response to society's demands (conscripted military service).

Sources of healthy identity for men may also involve hazards that can drag us down. Jobs, for instance, can become a diversion to avoid something we don't want to do. And satisfying work can become workaholism, where boundaries between self and work blur. Compulsively overcommitting to our work, we end up causing harm to ourselves and those close to us. Workaholism is an especially seductive trap because it's linked so closely with high productivity, dedication, and sacrifice, all of which society smiles upon and generously rewards.

The same kinds of dangers exist for play. Play for men is often highly competitive, and at moderate levels it motivates accomplishment. Too often, though, it pushes us into risky choices and leaves us broken. Competition naturally involves comparison, and comparisons can threaten our egos. Such competition may demand blood and sacrifice, even to the point of putting physical well-being or life at risk.

Like so much of life, actions aren't always clearly good or bad. They can lead to a healthy identity, and they can also become cheap merit markers—gold stars that reward those who perform well in acceptable ways or demerits that crush those who do not measure up to society's standards of masculinity.

What is clear is that characterizing men primarily as people of action limits our understanding of who boys and men are and who we can become.

FOR CONVERSATION

1. Who are you? How much of your identity is based on the things you do?
2. What pressures have you experienced to define yourself by your occupation or abilities?
3. How would your identity be different if you were unable to perform the occupations or tasks that fill your life today?

CONNECTEDNESS

Don

We are relational human beings. In the Genesis 2 creation account, God declares while creating human beings, "It is not good for the [human] to be alone; I will make a fitting companion for it" (v. 18 *The Inclusive Bible*).

The whole Bible is a story of relationships. Indeed, all of human history is characterized by many kinds of human relationships. Children, from their earliest moments of life through adolescence, depend on strong bonds with their caregivers to develop a healthy self. The interaction of dependent children with responsive caregivers nurtures connectedness, dependability, and trust. These bonds allow children to feel safe exploring their surroundings because they know their parents or family will be there to protect and sustain them.

When parents offer love, encouragement, support, and instruction, they increase their children's confidence, success, knowledge, and sense of meaning. This ultimately assures the children that they are valuable to others. They become strong and independent adults, with a rich sense of identity, and they grow to understand themselves as separate from but interconnected with others. This gives them the ability to form healthy relationships and join in collaborative activities in a community.

It's common to assume that such nurture is more important for girls and women, but boys and men are no less in need of connection. They are also no less able—at least at birth—to experience healthy connection. Society's false assumptions about masculinity and differences between boys and girls can be like weeds interfering with the growth of young plants. Sometimes the reasons for stunted growth are obvious; other times, they're not so clear. In all cases, when the parts of us designed for healthy connecting are not nourished, our emotional IQ becomes stunted, setting us up for chaos and wounds in our relationships. This can lead to a vicious cycle of avoiding vulnerability and being crushed under additional hurts. As difficult as vulnerability can be, it is a must for human closeness and intimacy.

Too often, men are taught that we should not depend on others for our well-being, and we end up without skills to form and maintain healthy relationships. At the same time, we live with confusing longings to connect with others, and we struggle to satisfy these natural yearnings in relationships with other men and women, both in friendship and in more intimate forms.

When a man fails to prove his masculinity in intimate relationships, shame fueled by a learned sense of entitlement can trigger desperation and even violent attack on anyone—usually women—perceived to be the source of the humiliation. These unmet expectations are not just about sexual performance. They may be about having a "trophy" partner for others to see; about feeling admiration and sometimes deference or even fear from a particular other; about "conquering"; and about deep experiences of humiliation in so many ways that may lead to striking out at a particular person or at the world.

Men have very few socially acceptable places to turn to for support and growth regarding relationships. Our often-limited ability to tune in to and name our feelings leaves us emotionally distressed and lost. Weighed down by insecurity, loneliness, embarrassment, shame, and fear—on top of childhood wounds from neglectful or traumatic relationships—many of us search for ways to soothe our pain. We turn to readily available substances (drugs, alcohol, food) and activities (gambling, risk-taking, porn, sex, and even rage) to medicate our hurt and regulate socially unacceptable feelings. The resulting addictions, which occur much more often in men than in women, bring only fleeting relief and high costs for men and those around us.

FOR CONVERSATION

1. What are or have been the most important relationships in your life? What makes them important?
2. When have you experienced times of loneliness? How did or do you cope with this?
3. How comfortable are you being vulnerable with others?
4. What are the gifts and challenges for you of being connected with others?
5. What small steps can you take—or are you already taking—to connect meaningfully with others?

RECOGNITION

Don

We generally long to be valued by those around us, especially our family and friends. And we look for opportunities to impress others with our personalities and our abilities.

The quantity and quality of the recognition we receive feeds our soul. Warm and supportive responses, even a smile or a kind word from a stranger, inspire a sense of belonging and being valued. This brings out the best in us, encouraging us to recognize people around us in similar ways. Our hearts long especially for the powerful stabilizing impacts of recognition by our intimate partners.

Our understanding of what it means to be a man determines our values and behaviors. These, in turn, shape the kind of recognition we seek and receive from others. As boys watch their fathers and other men in their lives, they learn what it means to be a man, copying behaviors that bring affirmation from others.

While this need for recognition plays a powerful role in making our lives better, it can also be problematic if we fail to achieve the recognition we crave. If recognition is merit-based, failure to reach acceptable levels of merit—or to receive recognition for what we believe we deserve—can crush us. The resulting shame and humiliation can deflate our self-esteem and hope, leading to self-destructive coping behaviors such as addictions or isolation. For an increasing number of men, suicide has become a way out.

Some men turn inward or away from others in their shame. Others ratchet up their self-defense mechanisms by inflating their egos and acting in ways they hope will bring them expressions of appreciation. In an often-repeated pattern, men use escalating amounts of pressure, intimidation, and eventually violence to win recognition from others.

This is what's happening under the surface for a significant number of men who turn to violence as they seek recognition and react to perceived threats to their selfhood. When a man's sense of who he is comes from others' recognition rather than from inside himself, and when society gives permission and even honor to men who express their bravado aggressively, we should not be surprised when violence is the result.

These dynamics play out individually and collectively. Together, men pump each other up, egging one another on to prove their worth and value. Anyone who bucks the group's understandings, including challenging or undermining group standards of masculinity, is punished in some way. The brotherhood holds great power of both recognition and marginalization. Men who want to be included in the group might have to sacrifice their preferred way of being in order to be considered "one of the guys." The alternative is to be willing to go it alone or find another group that will provide the needed recognition.

FOR CONVERSATION

1. What are the indicators of acceptable masculinity in the circles you are part of? In the broader society around you?
2. Are you attracted to or put off by masculine forms of gaining recognition?
3. How has recognition you've gained or failed to receive affected your life?
4. How might Christianity offer an alternative vision for masculinity that would offer males a healthier point of reference?

MEANING

Don

The beliefs, values, and behaviors we associate with being a man—collectively known as masculinity—vary widely. Sometimes they support us in developing healthy emotions and relationships, and other times they undermine us. Both parents and society influence boys according to which of the expressions of masculinity they throw their weight behind. The resulting messages greatly affect a boy's understanding of what it means to live as a male. Male children and youth then accept these characteristics as their own in different ways and degrees, consciously or unconsciously. Living into these creates further meaning for them.

In the past half century, what it means to be a male in North American society has undergone an overhaul. Old assumptions and beliefs about male dominance and privilege have been directly challenged by women seeking equity and by marginalized people who have exposed injustices perpetrated especially by white male power.

Globalization has also brought considerable change through evolving social and economic trends. This change has blurred once-clear lines about masculine definition and behavior. One outcome for men is what might be called a "loss of job description."

In some sectors of society, these radical changes have stirred up a backlash from people who want to return to more traditional ways of being men. For others, the changes are making room for men to live outside the Man Box with greater freedom and creativity. Still others are simply overwhelmed and trying to find their way. Some organizations are asking whether changing social trends are also resulting in growing injustices toward men in areas such as child custody, access and support orders in family court, and incarceration and sentencing. These challenges to traditional masculinity provide opportunities for clarity, increased intentionality, and new understandings to emerge.

Christian beliefs and values are also a significant source of meaning for many men, not only in explicitly Christian communities and families but also residually in society at large in North America. Certain understandings about men's roles and responsibilities, especially relative to corresponding beliefs about women, have dominated expressions of masculinity through the centuries of European settlement in North America. A barrage of critique—both external (from secular sources and other religious traditions) and internal (from, for example, Christian feminist and queer theology)—against these traditional understandings has brought both resistance and embrace. A variety of organizations loosely fitting under the umbrella of the Christian men's movement represent a reassertion of traditional positions, calling men back to "real manhood."

Our ability as men to find meaning in the various areas of our lives and social contexts is critical to our identity. We live in a time of rapid change and ambiguity, and this demands that we, individually and collectively, diligently seek understanding. Christians believe that we do this through living as beloved children of God in community, with each generation discerning what this looks like for their time.

 FOR CONVERSATION

1. What are the most important sources of meaning in your life?
2. What troubles you the most about this time of change and ambiguity of meaning?
3. What gives you hope in this time of change and ambiguity?
4. What would it mean to you to live as a beloved son of God?

As section 2 ends, let's stop to notice what's happening with us. After a minute of silence, discuss:

- How are we experiencing our open conversations?
- What gifts, difficulties, or tensions do we notice?
- Where is God's Spirit at work within and among us?

Personal Challenges

In This Section

INTRODUCTION

Don

> *I do not understand my own actions. For I do not do what I want,*
> *but I do the very thing I hate.*
> **—Paul, Romans 7:15**

THE STORY OF THE FALL in Genesis 3 portrays Eve and Adam making a choice to defy God's command not to eat of the tree of good and evil. As a result, they become alienated from God, from each other, and from the paradise of the garden of Eden. These same outcomes continue to trouble us today, often bringing overwhelming challenges that lead to unsettledness, distress, and deep pain.

Parker Palmer, Quaker author and activist, says it this way:

> Heartbreak comes with the territory called being human. When love and trust fail us, when what once brought meaning goes dry, when a dream drifts out of reach, a devastating disease strikes, or someone precious to us dies, our hearts break and we suffer.
>
> What can we do with our pain? How might we hold it and work with it? How do we turn the power of suffering toward new life? The way we answer those questions is critical because *violence is what happens when we don't know what else to do with our suffering.*[1]

That last sentence bears repeating: "Violence is what happens when we don't know what else to do with our suffering." When I first read this, it struck me as such a profound statement of truth about our lives. The sentence would be just as true if we replaced the last word, *suffering*, with the word *fear*, or *shame*, or *uncertainty*, or any other of the difficult emotions we humans experience.

We need to recognize that violence, as Palmer writes, is "not limited to inflicting physical harm. We do violence every time we violate the sanctity of the human self—our own or another person's."[2]

For men, this becomes especially relevant in three ways:

Many men do not know what to do with difficult emotions. They've been schooled in traditional male stoicism, which does not nurture healthy emotional intelligence. Boys and men need the permission and skills to participate fully in the rich and rewarding world of emotions. For this to happen, we have much work to do in breaking out of the box that restricts men's emotional health and well-being.

Men around the world are suffering. People who see only the relative privileges that society tends to give men might laugh at this statement. They might also say that our attention needs to be focused on the victims of men's violence. These are valid concerns that must be addressed, including acknowledgment that some of the destructive behavior of men is a reaction against much-needed changes. At the same time, men living with privilege and power often struggle intensely with an inner chaos and deep insecurities. When their experience of suffering is not heard or understood, it can tragically deepen their suffering. This, in turn, can lead to the further suffering of others.

Violence is a widespread response to this emotional turmoil.[3] Men, especially in North American society, are often given permission to be violent. Sometimes we are even celebrated for violent responses. So it's not surprising that many men default to violence in the absence of a more fully developed toolbox of life skills.

As you work through this section, consider these questions: How do we deal with difficult challenges in ways that bring healing and hope? How do we build resilience so that these challenges of life strengthen and deepen our experiences of being human rather than send us to difficult places and lead to the destruction of ourselves or others?

GRIEF

Don

We grieve because we love. We grieve because we have valued the presence of someone we felt connected to who is no longer present with us. We grieve at the loss of something that has had a special place in our lives or that we anticipated would become an important part of our future—a dream, a possession, an opportunity, an experience, a job, a role, a pet. The only thing more tragic than grief is feeling nothing in the face of loss.

Grief can be overwhelming, especially when what we've lost is of great value or when we're already trying to cope with other challenges. These other challenges may include previous losses, mental illness, loneliness, or isolation. Although grief is often personal and our experience of grief is our own, grieving alone can add another level of pain.

Complex grief occurs when a loss coincides with other factors that make the experience of loss more intense or prolong it. Particularly tragic situations—like sudden or extended illness, natural disaster, an accident, violent criminal activity, or the death of a child—may change the normal course of grief.

Aging or illness can also trigger grief. When our body or mind takes a downhill turn, we become very aware of how frail life really is. As our sense of usefulness fades, we long for our previous gifts, talents, and strengths because, for most of us, being useful means we're valuable. When a man has to depend on others for what he used to be able to do himself, the experience of vulnerability can be especially troubling and sometimes humiliating.

While grief is difficult for everyone, it can be extra complex for men. The surge of raw emotion in the face of loss can be extremely difficult to handle if we're struggling to be comfortable with our emotions or to even just tune in to them. Messages about the importance of male independence and strength can leave us confused about our deep feelings of loss. What do such feelings mean, we wonder, about our dependency on the person who is now no longer in our life?

This dependency might have filled our needs simply on a practical, daily-life level. When we lose a person, it may be that the person filled deep and extremely important emotional and relational needs in our life. This latter situation is more difficult for some men to acknowledge and to believe that people might understand. Many of us have been taught not to need (not to be "needy"), but our human longings for connection and recognition (see the Human Needs section) are closely tied to the relationships we hold dear. Grief is a natural response to the end of those relationships.

Healthy grieving happens when we acknowledge our pain and allow time to shift the intensity of our feelings and our perspective about our loss. Healthy grieving means we allow our memories and our sadness to shape who we are this side of the loss. The idea that we "get over it" cheapens our humanity and the value of what we have lost. Attempts to minimize, avoid, or rush our way through the experience of loss generally lead to prolonged and, too often, crippling effects of grief. Unaddressed grief can haunt lives for years to come.

Seeking support from significant people in our lives, including faith partners, can be invaluable on our journeys. This is especially the case when our need to be honest with our own feelings of loss brings us into new and uncharted territory in our lives.

 FOR CONVERSATION

1. What losses have you had in your life? What have those experiences of loss been like for you?
2. What has enabled, or hindered, healthy grieving for you or for others you have witnessed grieving?

FAILURE

Don

We live in a world obsessed with success. Doing things well and succeeding often form a major part of our self-identity as well as how we are seen by others. We easily become consumed by chasing after success, by reaching the markers that indicate success, and then by maintaining our status of being successful. This generally does not happen without a cost to ourselves, to others—including our spouses and families—and even to society.

Success is highly competitive and is often a zero-sum game. Few reach the mountaintops, and many play supporting roles that can be dehumanizing and hazardous to health and well-being. And when the climb up the ladder toward our goals of achievement challenges our values or our preferred way of living, we are faced with a dilemma: Do we compromise our preferred ways of living—who we want to be—or do we let go of our goals as we had envisioned them?

Success can also be defined as meeting the basic expectations of life that we take upon ourselves or that are put on us by others. These expectations have changed throughout the centuries. Traditionally, men have been expected to carry the responsibility of providing for and protecting families and communities. Men have also been expected to lead and to be competent in other areas of life. In many ways, this is still true, although the messages today from family, religious, and cultural norms are more varied about the roles we "should" fill as successful men.

Learning how to be discerning about which of these messages we let in is of utmost importance because these expectations become part of us. Failure, then, becomes falling short of these expectations. This often drives men into difficult places and contributes to emotional and mental deterioration, isolation, apathy, addictions, or even suicide.

Sometimes our experience of failure is temporary, such as the loss of a job when other employment options are available. At other times, failure is (or at least seems to be) permanent, and the consequences are greater.

Attempts to avoid failure can be equally great. For instance, taking on hazardous or thankless work to support families regardless of whether it matches one's actual gifts, abilities, or interests can leave a man feeling disposable. Stepping into a heroic role that carries a risk of violence in order to gain the praise of others or for financial reward can take a heavy toll. Too many men find themselves broken, wasted by years of attempting to follow society's prescription for success.

We have the opportunity as individuals, and as a society, to radically change how we measure success. This includes deciding whether "success" as we have known it is even a useful concept in our lives. For starters, we must work toward change that values all persons unconditionally. We must also encourage and nurture opportunities for all people to use their gifts and abilities in meaningful ways that make their own lives better while contributing to the well-being of their families and society. We must continue finding ways to share the responsibilities of supporting and protecting each other.

 FOR CONVERSATION

1. What does it mean to you to be a successful man in terms of the roles you play or your employment? What do you wish it would mean?
2. How do you think people of other genders in your social circles would answer the above questions about men's roles?
3. What successes or failures have you experienced in your life? How have these affected how you view yourself?
4. What has allowed you to navigate failure in healthy ways, and what has hindered your progress? How do you see the markers of success and failure changing in our society?

SHAME

Don

To speak of shame, I will turn to my favorite shame researcher and fellow social worker, Brené Brown. Brown defines shame as "the intensely painful feeling or experience of believing that we are flawed and therefore unworthy of love and belonging."[4] Living with or in shame goes deeper than dealing with behaviors, shortcomings, and errors. Shame strikes at the center of who we are, telling us we are flawed and unworthy at our very core and that this awful reality can never change, because it's just the way we are. Shame leaves us feeling that there is no way out other than medicating our pain or looking for someone or something to unload our self-loathing on.

Believing that masculinity must be proven and maintained through performance, men are especially prone to the effects of shame. As Brown writes, shame for men means failure, being wrong, defective, soft, weak, fearful. When we're ridiculed or called out for any of these things, it's like a strong punch to the gut. "Basically," Brown writes, "men live under the pressure of one unrelenting message: Do not be perceived as weak."[5] This fear of being seen as weak is not just in the eyes of other men. It is also the fear of being seen as inadequate by women—mothers, sisters, colleagues, friends, girlfriends, wives, daughters.

Shame can also lurk constantly around the corner, threatening to reveal less desirable realities about us. If we are carrying a sense of deep inadequacy or regret about previous behaviors, we might well live in fear that we will be discovered as less, much less, than we are perceived by those who matter to us. This is sometimes called "imposter syndrome"—fearing that one will be found out to be a fraud, a poser. Someone like the wizard in *The Wizard of Oz* who hides his inadequacy behind a curtain and a loudspeaker. An invitation to be vulnerable or real in the face of such fears feels like a mountain that's too high and dangerous to climb, and it can drive men further from relationship.

Identifying the difference between guilt and shame, and between healthy and unhealthy guilt, can be helpful. Whereas shame is a feeling of being flawed at one's core and unworthy of love, guilt is the feeling that creeps in after doing something against values or expectations. When those values have been imposed by others and run against our own values, or when the expectations are unreasonable, our feelings of guilt will ultimately be unhealthy. When the values and expectations are reasonable and held by people we value, or match our own preferred ways of being, then our resulting guilt can inspire healing and needed change.

Shame is strong. It can undermine courage, connection, and vulnerability. But it cannot endure self-compassion and honesty, especially when practiced in the loving embrace of true relationship. When someone welcomes us with an open heart and affirms our worthiness, it unlocks a door to share honestly about the things that are most difficult to face about ourselves. When we speak our shame in the presence of that welcoming other, shame's power over our life withers.

Bryan Stevenson says in his book *Just Mercy: A Story of Justice and Redemption:* "Each of us is more than the worst thing we've ever done."[6] In Stevenson's work with some of the most marginalized people of society, this belief has anchored his pursuit of mercy and grace where it is in terribly short supply. I hope that people I meet in my clinical practice experience in my presence an opportunity to begin to believe, in deep and healing ways, that they, too, are much more than the worst they've experienced about themselves.

God invites us to know that the "more" we can hold on to about our essence is that we are children of God, unconditionally loved by our Creator. Our status, regardless of our failures, is rooted in who God is and how God holds us!

FOR CONVERSATION

1. What difference does it make for you to distinguish shame from guilt?
2. Where in your life or the lives of other men do you see the concept of imposter syndrome and the fear of being discovered?
3. Have you ever experienced unconditional love and forgiveness? How might resting in God's unconditional love and forgiveness wither shame that you carry?
4. How might your friendship with other men invite them to experience release from shame?

PRIDE

Don

The concept of pride has a mixed history in our human story, containing polar opposite uses of the word.

On one hand, pride has been expressed as conceit, excessive self-esteem, elevated image of self. This kind of pride leads to disdain and condescension toward others. It relies heavily on comparison and competition, and it may be highly threatened when shown up by someone else's positive characteristic. This type of pride is also fragile. It causes anxiety and may demand a lot of energy to stay at the top of the pecking order. It may also lead to attempts to eliminate the competition, even to the point of violence.

On the other hand, pride can be based on a reasonable level of self-respect that grows from being delighted in or affirmed for accomplishments. When a youngster catches the fly ball to end the championship game and the crowd cheers, or when the shy contestant on *America's Got Talent* wows the judges and receives the Golden Buzzer, pride lights up their face. Watching them, our hearts swell. Who would want to take that moment away from anyone?

Within Christian tradition, pride is one of the seven deadly sins. Some consider it the deadliest of all. Proverbs 16:18, an often-quoted verse, warns: "Pride goes before destruction, and a haughty spirit before a fall." The original sin of Eve and Adam is attributed to their choice to follow their own will (pride) over following God.

Historically, Christians have emphasized the lowliness of human nature, cautioning against anything that would decrease awareness of the sinfulness of our basic nature in the presence of a lofty and holy God. As we focused on the importance of our spiritual selves, we became wary of our human needs, and any form of pride based on our own achievements became suspect. I grew up, for instance, with stories of my paternal grandparents being very cautious about giving my father verbal affirmations lest he develop a "swelled head."

It's a dance between the dangers of an exaggerated yet delicate self-image and the need to hold ourselves with self-respect and esteem—a dance that creates confusion and uncertainty for many. Characteristics and accomplishments that "prove" our masculinity are too often the only footholds some of us have for believing we are worthy or have status in the world worth living for. As fragile as these footholds are, in the absence of more-solid ground for a sense of self, many men hang on to them for dear life. Sometimes literally.

What is the healthy alternative to this danger-filled place of pride? If our sense of personal well-being is based on what value we've earned in this world, we are in trouble. But if we can see ourselves as children of God—created in God's image and loved unconditionally—we are released from the nonstop effort to prove our worth. As Gareth Brandt writes in *Under Construction*, "The experiential knowledge that we are deeply and unconditionally loved is at the core of male spirituality. To be loved is the ground of all human spirituality, but it is particularly poignant for men."[7]

Micah 7:18 says that God delights in showing unfailing and constant loving-kindness to us. May God's nonstop loving-kindness toward you be the anchor of your well-being!

FOR CONVERSATION

1. What's the difference between conceit and affirming your abilities or achievements?
2. In what ways have you pursued pride based on your merits—your personal characteristics or accomplishments?
3. How is it freeing—or perhaps difficult—for you to receive unmerited, unconditional love as God's beloved?
4. When have you affirmed others—or received affirmation from others—for genuine gifts or accomplishments? How did this affect you or the other person or persons?

ANXIETY

Don

Anxiety is the experience of fear or apprehension about an anticipated event or situation. At a basic level, it is a normal and healthy reaction to stress or threat. If we sense a threat to our well-being, anxiety alerts us to get ready, and our brain generates hormones—sometimes even without our conscious awareness of threat—triggering our body's preparation for fight or flight. Without such systems of warning, we would be considerably more vulnerable in the world.

This type of anxiety, though, is not what we generally think of when we consider the impacts of anxiety on ourselves, the people we care about, or the society around us. Regardless of whether anxiety is increasing in society, it definitely is more openly acknowledged, and its impacts are being identified more fully. The impact of anxiety in some groups of people, particularly children and teenagers, is raising much concern and is the focus of research and intervention.

Anxiety is not one size fits all; it affects people in very different ways. That said, several factors are commonly associated with anxiety, including depression; post-traumatic stress disorder; the effects of chemicals such as caffeine, alcohol, and marijuana; and triggering events such as stress and risk. Signs of anxiety include physical sensations such as rapid heart rate, sweaty palms, or nausea, and psychological indicators such as racing thoughts and feelings of doom. The intensity of anxiety can go from nuisance to incapacitating.

The power of anxiety to negatively affect our life depends on our capacity to respond to threats, whether real or perceived. When a threat is rising faster than our ability to cope, we will feel more anxious. High levels of anxiety may require professional help, and psychotropic medication may be prescribed to bring relief.

Men, however, are often reluctant to seek such help. The belief that we should be able to successfully meet any challenge and face any threat means that any experience of anxiety can be very unsettling for us and even a source of shame. As a result, men's anxiety often goes untreated. One of the outcomes of anxiety for men is higher rates of addiction and suicide.

For those who can gather strength and support in the face of challenges, anxiety may well disappear. In my work with clients, I generally describe anxiety as something to be managed through increased understanding, self-care, and better coping methods. I don't talk about curing anxiety, because doing so could set people up for disappointment if they experience lingering effects of anxiety.

Matthew 11:28–30 is an invitation to find rest, which is so needed for those who suffer from anxiety: "Come to me, all you who are weary and are carrying heavy burdens, and I will give you rest. Take my yoke upon you, and learn from me; for I am gentle and humble in heart, and you will find rest for your souls. For my yoke is easy, and my burden is light." Though not a cure-all or a guarantee of healing, this verse affirms God's gentle presence and God's will for us to find rest along the way.

FOR CONVERSATION

1. What occasions in your life produce anxiety?
2. In your experience, what helps relieve anxiety?
3. What does rest look like in your life?
4. How might you respond to someone who is experiencing anxiety?

ANGER

Don

Anger can be a difficult topic for men. The experience of anger may feel like walking through a minefield, with trouble—sometimes life-changing trouble—just one step away. We may also feel defensive at the bad press that men's anger gets. Regardless of whether all the negative press is deserved, without a doubt we have much work to do on changing behaviors related to anger, for the sake of those we love, for our communities, and also for ourselves.

As an emotion, anger is an internal state that arises in response to stimuli related to experiences of insecurity, fear, unsettledness, disempowerment, injustice, and impending risk to ourselves or people, institutions, beliefs, or values we feel compelled to protect. Though anger is an instinctual emotion, not everyone gets angry about the same things. Especially when it comes to matters of personal offense or social justice, anger is closely tied to our values and expectations. We get angry when something we feel strongly about is violated. This may include our personal physical safety or the safety of a loved one. Or it may be about our expectation that a referee be a superhuman who nails every single call (especially when doing so benefits our team) or that the person we are attracted to should respond in a certain way to our advances.

A more hidden reality that triggers much male anger is, ironically, that men often experience great fear, insecurity, and powerlessness. Underdeveloped emotional intelligence—and, for many men, deeply wounded selves—can make relating to others very intimidating and overwhelming, especially when vulnerability is required. Anger is generally the only permitted and familiar emotional response, and for many it's the only tool available to fend off perceived threats. Tragically, men too often direct their anger inward in deep experiences of shame, contributing to their high rates of addiction and suicide.

Yet anger is part of our human experience. Note that Ephesians 4:26 assumes this to be the case: "Be angry but do not sin." The difficulty arises in how we handle ourselves as men in the midst of anger. In John 2, Jesus' forceful actions suggest he was angered by the money changers in the temple. Moved by that anger, he sought a remedy to the unjust practices in his Father's house.

Anger as a warning system and as the energy that drives creative, meaningful change can actually be life-giving. For too long, men have had a very unhealthy relationship with anger, but the opportunities for transforming anger are great.

It's to everyone's benefit for us to work hard, individually and collectively, to learn to live well in our anger and with the full range of our emotions.

This leads to a final perspective on anger. Often, anger is not the issue. When anger follows a real or perceived threat to self or others, the greatest difficulty arises when men have only a hammer in their toolbox instead of refined skills of gentleness and wisdom. Men need to be able to tell the difference between emotional states so that anger doesn't consume all the other emotions. We need to know how to be present with our anger, allow it to dissipate, or harvest and direct it toward healthy resolution of the issue at hand without causing more damage to ourselves and others.

FOR CONVERSATION

1. In what ways has anger negatively affected your life—as a recipient of another person's anger or as someone who has expressed anger?
2. How might it be helpful to become more self-aware of how anger develops in us—to see the progression from trigger event to thoughts, then to emotions, and ultimately to actions?
3. We often hear "That's just how men are" in discussions about anger. How would you respond to such a statement?
4. The Ephesians passage noted earlier reads, "Be angry but do not sin." What is your understanding of this verse? How do you see sin as related to anger? How do Jesus' actions in clearing the temple relate to this discussion?

GREED

Don

Greed is a compulsive seeking to accumulate possessions or power. Greed arises from a fear of deficiency or a sense of deserving more than one's share of wealth or influence. It leads to ignoring the plight of others and to refusing personal responsibility for the impacts of one's actions. From a perspective of scarcity, greed grasps for limited commodities, believing in the right to accumulate as much as one can regardless of the effect on others. In a broad sense, inequity in economic well-being, social power, and privilege exposes the threads of human greed snaking throughout much of society.

For some Christians, the cloak of a prosperity gospel—the belief that God wills and rewards wealth to those who find favor in God's eyes—is a fitting cover to justify greed. But Luke 12:15 records this warning by Jesus: "Take care! Be on your guard against all kinds of greed, for one's life does not consist in the abundance of possessions." And 1 Corinthians 6:10 names the greedy in a list that also includes thieves, drunkards, revilers, and robbers, indicating that "none of these will inherit the kingdom of God"—strong words of sanction against greed!

Men have often been handed the task of accumulating provisions for their families, but how much to gather and how to do this have not always been clear. The male ego has too often been socialized to take a competitive stance, where the more a person earns the more valuable they and their family become. Showing off one's toys, competing with neighbors or peers, and dreaming of the next pursuit is intoxicating for some men.

But the costs and risks of greed can be devastating. Failure to keep up with others can be a source of shame and embarrassment. And workaholism resulting from a drive to accumulate can have a significant negative impact on family relationships and personal health. It also holds no guarantee of financial success, especially in a time of economic volatility.

There's a classic illustration of the risk that comes with greed. It begins with a traditional monkey trap where bait is placed in a hole in a secured coconut or branch just big enough for an open monkey hand to reach in. But when the monkey grabs the bait, it can't pull its hand out of the hole. Unwilling to let go, the monkey is trapped and captured! We are often like monkeys unwilling to let go. As Norman Grubb writes, "For *what we take, in fact takes us.*"[8]

Powerful practices that counteract greed include humility and generosity. The deep wisdom of the biblical call for us to do good and share what we have (Hebrews 13:16) benefits not only those on the receiving end of our actions but also anyone who follows that call.

 FOR CONVERSATION

1. What do you want to grab? What are you greedy for?
2. To what extent does what you grab, grab you?
3. When does the responsibility to provide for yourself or your family become a compulsion toward greed?
4. How do you pay attention to greed in your financial decisions?
5. Do you share these decisions with anyone in a relationship of accountability?

VULNERABILITY

Don

Of all the discussions in this book, the topic of vulnerability may be one of the more difficult, and maybe the most important. There is little that goes more against the grain of traditional masculinity than the concept of vulnerability. In fact, much of what is generally taught to boys and men about being men is designed to limit vulnerability and fine-tune "strength." How do we reconcile our understandings of healthy strength and determination that serve our humanity well with the absolute-must relational requirements of vulnerability?

"Vulnerability is the core, the heart, the center, of meaningful human experiences," writes Brené Brown.[9] If this is true, given the opposite messages men have been receiving about power and strength, how have we managed until now? Are we in a different time and place that might allow us to embrace vulnerability in a new way as men? Is it an either/or, or might it be some combination of both? And what might that look like?

Vulnerability refers to the condition of being exposed to potential attack or harm, either physically or emotionally. Of the two, physical vulnerability might be easier to understand because the need for self-protection is likely clearer. Self-defense training improves our chances for physical well-being. For many men, owning firearms is the epitome of feeling safe from any threat.

Emotional vulnerability is a totally different arena. It's a place of risk that leaves us open to pain and disappointment. Therefore many men simply avoid it. Maybe sometimes by conscious choice but more likely because closing the door to our vulnerability is what we learned growing up. But this just creates a new problem; avoiding experiences of powerlessness or appearing weak makes emotional sharing difficult.

Emotional vulnerability, according to Brown, is "the cradle of the emotions and experiences that we crave. Vulnerability is the birthplace of love, belonging, joy, courage, empathy, and creativity. It is the source of hope, empathy, accountability, and authenticity."[10] Our ability to connect, belong, and love is made possible by our ability to open ourselves to each other, to let down our guard, to be truly willing to give and receive vulnerably. But life often leaves us reluctant to expose ourselves, especially if we have been wounded by previous experiences of sharing ourselves openly.

The surprise of healthy vulnerability is that it's actually an outcome of a certain kind of strength. When we know who we are as God's beloved and that our worth comes from the fact that God created us, we can more easily dare to show our true selves. We are not perfect in our belovedness, but God's love for us, thankfully, is unconditional.

Healthy vulnerability also goes hand in hand with healthy boundaries. The ability to manage healthy boundaries—to know how and when to limit others' capacities to disrespect or harm us—will enable us to be fully present with those who do offer us their loving and nurturing presence. We are called to a journey of healing and growth in relationship with others, and this journey is enriched when we do it with a willingness to give to and receive from one another in our vulnerability.

Movement toward honest and open sharing of ourselves invites the same from others. Our most intimate relationships offer mutuality and the assurance that we will be welcomed and comforted even in our brokenness. We cannot achieve this without a willingness to be "naked and unashamed" in the presence of the other.

FOR CONVERSATION

1. What makes it difficult to be vulnerable?
2. When have you been vulnerable, but maybe just didn't admit it? What was that like for you?
3. Men commonly learn that being strong means not being vulnerable. In what ways is this true or not true to your experience?

EMPATHY

Don

Learning and practicing the skills of both offering and receiving empathy can be one of the most transformative experiences for men. The subtle but harmful messages of independence and invulnerability that men receive from society too often numb us to the ability to tune in well to our own and others' lives, to experience knowing and being fully known by others.

Empathy is the quality of entering into the experiences of others to see things from their perspective, "to put ourselves in their shoes." To open up to such an encounter, we must tune in to our own feelings that arise in the presence of another person's emotions. We must also face our own thoughts and emotions to really pay attention to the other person's unique perspective. This requires staying focused on the other's situation and listening to our intuition of how that situation has most likely affected them. It calls for opening our emotional selves to tune in to the other's emotional experience, and our minds to understand that experience.

When listening to another person's troubles, we must restrain ourselves from quick and pat responses; too often our go-to as men is to follow an impulse to jump in with a response that tries to fix or quickly soothe a situation. Rather, we must stay in the moment, as uncomfortable as that might be, and our best initial response may well be silence. A beautiful term for this moment is "holding space" for the other. Active listening, and then reflecting back to the person that we are in touch with their experience, lets the other know that they are being heard and that we are holding their sharing with the respectful kindness it deserves.

Gently asking clarifying (not probing) questions about how another person is feeling in the moment may also give that person a chance to process their situation further. Once a strong, supporting, empathic connection is created, there may be opportunity for additional conversation where ideas and wisdom about moving forward might arise. But this needs to be done with sensitivity to the needs of the other and one's own tendencies to potentially overwhelm and dominate a situation, possibly to avoid one's own discomfort.

Being on the receiving end of empathy may be a rare experience for men. This is especially true because men usually do not have the kind of friendships with each other that are open enough to have deeply empathic conversations.

Empathy may plainly feel uncomfortable for men because it requires the vulnerability of being sensitively heard and seen by another person. Opening up to, and receiving, such tenderness and sensitivity is another practice that men have an opportunity to learn. Giving and receiving empathy requires practice, and like a muscle, it strengthens with use and atrophies when left idle.

In my ten years of clinical practice, which now has a significant focus on services to men, I have been privileged to experience the power of empathy in men's lives. Being present in open and positive ways to men's stories has provided the space for them to feel heard in unique and profound ways. The safety created by this way of being present invites honest self-reflection and emotional vulnerability. It also nurtures the kind of self-image that can inspire hope and lead to change.[11] Unfortunately, many men never have this opportunity. Instead, they stay stuck in isolation and unhealthy patterns of life.

Whether through the presence of a true friend or through a "paid professional friend," as one of my clients calls me, the experience of empathy can be life-giving.

FOR CONVERSATION

1. Are you a "fixer"? When have you experienced someone trying to fix problems in your life?
2. What experiences have you had where "fixing" got in the way of giving or receiving empathy?
3. What experiences have you had of receiving empathy from others? Of being fully heard without judgment? What was this like for you?
4. What tools do you use (or have you experienced others using) to listen to yourself or others without judgment?

PREJUDICE

Steve

A woman once said to me, "Steve, you don't know how hard it is to live in Goshen [Indiana] as a poor, Puerto Rican lesbian with a biracial child."

I thought our community was a nice place to live. It is for me—as a white, middle-class, heterosexual, and married man with a family. But I don't have to deal with what she does. I don't even have to think about this, because I'm part of the dominant culture of this place, whereas she's not.

This conversation made me wonder how people mistreat her because of her differences. And it invited me to examine what prejudices I have and how I express them in ways I may not be aware of. After all, we all have implicit bias—stereotypes and attitudes that unconsciously affect how we understand and act toward other people.

How we look at people influences how we relate to them. Thus, it's important to become aware of how we view people who are different from us and how this affects our relationships with them. One of the ways we can work at this is being clear in our use of words such as prejudice, discrimination, and social isms like sexism and racism.

Let's define what these words mean and how they relate (see table).

Prejudice	Negative (pre)judgment of what we think and feel about groups of people different from us; a disposition.
Discrimination	How we treat groups of people based on our prejudice; a behavior.
Oppression	Controlling and denying something of value based on the group to which one belongs.
Privilege	Having (1) unearned benefits because of the group to which one belongs, and (2) power to impose one's prejudice on others to benefit one's group.

Consciously or unconsciously, all of us have some prejudices toward others with certain differences. Those differences may include age, sex, race, ethnicity, culture, class, religion, sexual orientation, education, and ability. While anyone can mistreat others, only those with power can impose their prejudice to discriminate against or oppress others. Unless we address this reality, group prejudice plus systemic power to discriminate leads to social isms like sexism, racism, heterosexism, ageism, ableism, and classism.[12]

Jesus confronted social problems in his day by crossing boundaries to relate with others different from him and by calling his followers to love all people regardless of color, class, creed, or deed. We see this when Jesus is with the woman at the well (John 4:1–30). In the minds of those in the dominant Hebrew culture, the woman had three strikes against her and was "out": (1) she was a woman, (2) she was a Samaritan, and (3) she'd had five husbands. Instead of focusing on these issues, however, Jesus looked at her as a beloved daughter of God, spoke to her with respect, and received water from her, to the astonishment of his disciples.

James learned from his brother Jesus to recognize and confront prejudice. In his letter, James calls out prejudice that's partial to one group over another. He highlights the inequities between telling a person in fine clothes, "Have a seat here," and saying to someone who is poor, "Stand over there." "Have you not made distinctions among yourselves," James asks, "and become judges with evil thoughts?" He then calls people to live by the royal law: "You shall love your neighbor as yourself" (see James 2:1–8).

As James points out, the problem involves buying into social distinctions that make some people seem more valuable than others, and supporting social patterns that enable these judgments to be practiced. So let's pay attention to our thoughts and actions and how we participate in social patterns that keep injustices alive, remembering that all people are beloved children of God, created in the divine image, and that we are all members together in one human family.

> For other important definitions to consider, see **"Terms to Understand, Issues to Address"**; for an exercise, consider **"The Male Privilege Checklist"**—both at bit.ly/ LivingThatMatters.

FOR CONVERSATION

1. What prejudices do you notice within you and in the culture around you?
2. How have these prejudices influenced how you relate to others?
3. How have you practiced or experienced discrimination?
4. What has been your experience of privilege or oppression?

COMPULSIONS

Don

We generally assume our actions are a result of our conscious choices. Based on previous experience, we first consider our options in response to stimuli, then we make the selection we think has the best chance of bringing about whatever we hope will happen. Much of life fits this model. There is, though, a set of behaviors with a less clear cause-and-effect process. We call these compulsions. Sometimes we act with compulsion, from habit, without thinking about the potential hurt resulting to ourselves, our loved ones, or society.

Compulsive and addictive actions are external behaviors that we use to help manage what's going on inside us. These activities may distract from less desirable realities, soothe unwanted emotional states, and create a sense of empowerment to counteract experiences of powerlessness and helplessness. And these core motivations are generally not immediately available to our consciousness. Because the nature of impulses is convoluted and often hidden, persons consumed by such behaviors may not appear logical.

Paul in Romans 7:15–20 expresses exasperation about his own struggles with unwanted impulses that overwhelm his best intentions. Many of us, in public or private ways, know this struggle well; in most categories of life, men experience higher rates of addiction than women. They also die of addiction-related conditions in greater numbers. Alcohol, cigarettes, drugs, sex, and pornography are more obvious addictions. Workaholism and obsessive working out are also problematic for men, though these activities get rewarded socially and are therefore often mistaken as positive pursuits. Compulsive gaming is a newer and potent addiction, especially for young men.

In a society highly motivated by avoidance of pain, dissonance, or any troubling emotional state, we are easily influenced to try whatever offers a shortcut to a state of relative peace. Like a painkiller, the ability to numb discomfort is highly attractive. But also like a painkiller, if we simply numb pain we may fail to understand the cause of the pain and to find legitimate and lasting ways to heal the underlying issues. We may even cause more damage because we don't hear the messages the pain is sending us that something is not operating in a healthy manner.

Emotional pain can stem from past wounds we've ignored, years of unsuccessful piled-up attempts to heal those wounds, or current overwhelming life circumstances. The reality for many men is that unhealed wounds of the past make it very hard to deal with current stressors. A history of avoiding difficult emotions through addictions makes it more likely a man will continue along such a path unless he recognizes what he's doing and deliberately chooses to take a road to recovery. A helpful question is not "Why the addiction?" but rather "Why the pain?" Genetically inherited predispositions may also play a role in compulsions and addictions.

Healing or managing compulsions and addictions calls for two things: (1) addressing one's capacity to face the uncomfortable emotions, and (2) developing options for coping that are focused more on healing the causes than on avoiding the pain.

This may require medical support, a twelve-step recovery program like Alcoholics Anonymous or Celebrate Recovery, or the support of friends who can come around and provide care and accountability. Rarely do we overcome compulsions and addictions by only solitary practices.

FOR CONVERSATION

1. What compulsive or addictive tendencies do you identify in your life?
2. How do you manage these?
3. How do you address underlying emotions and needs beneath your compulsions?
4. What practices help you experience freedom from compulsion?
5. How have you been affected by the compulsions or addictions of others in your life?

As section 3 ends, let's stop to notice what's happening with us. After a minute of silence, discuss:

- How are we experiencing our open conversations?
- What gifts, difficulties, or tensions do we notice?
- Where is God's Spirit at work within and among us?

Sexual Wholeness

In This Section

Sexuality

Embodiment

Eros

Integrity

Confession

Vision

Orientation

Identities

Intimacy

Fidelity

INTRODUCTION

Steve

> *Eat, O friends, and drink: drink deeply, O lovers!*
> **—Song of Songs 5:1 RSV**

THIS SECTION FOCUSES on various aspects of sexual wholeness. This is a challenging issue for most men, and few of us ever talk about our struggles. As a result, many of us carry our burdens alone. In this section, we invite men to break their silence and share with one another in order to experience God's healing power of love in community.

We begin by defining sexuality as something more than sex. While *sex* is simply one syllable, *sexuality* has five syllables—suggesting how much richer sexuality is meant to be in our lives. In God's design, sexuality and spirituality are related to each other in that both desire intimate union. As such, sexuality is a good and beautiful gift from God for us to enjoy.

In the next topic, we recognize that we are embodied sexual beings. From the beginning, God meant for us to be "naked and . . . not ashamed" (Genesis 2:25) and to embrace our bodies—genitals and all—as good. We also turn to eros, or erotic love, as something good to affirm. Referring to the Song of Songs, with its erotic desire and unveiled imagery, we celebrate the passionate expression of sexual love. We also point to the call in Proverbs 5 to enjoy sexual intimacy within a right relationship.

After affirming the gift of sexuality, we focus on sexual integrity, not only in terms of uprightness but also in terms of wholeness. In this session, we call us to get our stuff together so that sex and sexuality, sexuality and spirituality, body and spirit are held together. God desires this integrated wholeness for our relationships for our own happiness and well-being.

We then turn to confession as a part of sexual integrity. As another word for truth-telling, confession invites honesty in sharing with a loving God, ourselves, and others how we struggle and fall short in our sexuality. Vulnerability like this is hard for many men because it often involves a sense of shame or weakness. But when we practice this together, we realize we are not alone; we are in good company with others who struggle—including Paul, who in Romans 7 admits his own difficult struggle.

Next we turn to vision—that is, how we see others. This is critical, for how we look at others influences how we relate to them. To correct our lust-distorted vision, we call men to recognize that all people—no matter their gender—are beloved children of God created in the divine image. Here we call attention to the common struggle many men have with pornography.

After that, we introduce sexual orientation and gender identities. These concerns have been a source of considerable difficulty in our lives and in the church. In these sessions, we define the issues and offer questions for conversation. Under the topic of sexual orientation, we describe a range of experiences that gay men encounter and pose a question about same-sex marriage. Within gender identity, we discuss coming to terms with the reality that not everyone fits in the boxes of either male or female.

We close this section on sexual wholeness with reflections on intimacy and fidelity. We take the description of the first couple being naked and unashamed as an expression of not only innocence and purity but also the intimacy that God intends. Here we see intimacy as being fully seen and known without judgment or fear. This is the intimate knowing and union we desire.

Finally, we take a look at fidelity, focusing on God's call for faithfulness in our sexual behavior and covenant relationships. With society's changing understandings of sexuality and relationships, defining fidelity is increasingly difficult. Nevertheless, we reconsider what fidelity means for sexual wholeness and invite us to examine how we honor fidelity in our lives.

> For exercises and additional material, refer to what's available at bit.ly/LivingThatMatters.

SEXUALITY

Steve

A journalist once asked, Why are men so consumed by sex? "Did nature simply overload us in the mating department, hot-wiring us for the sex that is so central to the survival of the species, and never mind the sometimes sloppy consequences? Or is there something smarter and subtler at work, some larger interplay among sexuality, life and what it means to be human?"[1]

We answer, "Both." As animals, most of us are hardwired with a sex drive for mating. As humans, we are also designed by God with a desire for intimacy, which can include sex. Both are true and create a dynamic tension within us as we experience a primitive drive to unite with physical body as well as a deeper spiritual desire to connect with another person.[2] Both of these are part of our God-given impulse to "become one flesh" (Genesis 2:24). God created sex not only for procreation but also for pleasure and intimacy in a secure, loving relationship where these are most fully enjoyed.[3]

As the words themselves demonstrate, sex is part of sexuality. And sexuality and spirituality also belong together. They share a common longing for union with another.[4] But these two ways of being are often split apart, especially by men.

Consider two stories told at a Mennonite Men retreat on sexuality:

STORY 1: A husband and wife in their forties were together in a cottage at a spiritual retreat center. The woman, feeling especially close to her husband in their shared spiritual experience, asked him if he wanted to have sex. "Here?" he asked. Having been taught that "sex is dirty, save it for marriage," he didn't think a place of prayer was appropriate for sex. His wife, however, who understood spirituality and sexuality as belonging together, helped her husband see that this was a good time and place to be intimate together. So her husband tried to have sex, but with his split view of sexual and spiritual intimacy hovering over him, he struggled to have an erection and reach orgasm.

STORY 2. At another spiritual retreat center, an older couple in their seventies were together. They, too, felt unusually intimate in the place. The man shared how they pulled their twin beds together in their guest room. As they were having sex, the beds split apart and dumped the couple on the floor. Unhurt, they laughed together about what happened and noted that in the future they needed to bring clamps to hold the beds together! Months later as they set out for the retreat center again, the wife asked her husband, "Did you remember to bring the clamps?"

In this lovely case, the couple's clamped beds illustrate healthy intimacy, where spirituality and sexuality are joined.

In *The Holy Longing*, Ronald Rolheiser makes a helpful distinction between genitality and sexuality while at the same time holding them together:

> *Genitality*, having sex, is only one aspect of that larger reality of sexuality, albeit a very important one. . . .
>
> Sexuality is a beautiful, good, extremely powerful, sacred energy, given us by God and experienced in every cell of our being as an irrepressible urge to overcome our incompleteness, to move towards unity and consummation with that which is beyond us. It is also the pulse to celebrate, to give and to receive delight, to find our way back to the Garden of Eden where we can be naked, shameless, and without worry and work as we make love in the moonlight.[5]

Holding sexuality and spirituality together, Rolheiser offers this affirmation:

> *Sexuality* is an all-encompassing energy inside of us. In one sense, it is identifiable with the principle of life itself. It is the drive for love, communion, community, friendship, family, affection, wholeness, consummation, creativity, self-perpetuation, [immortality], joy, delight, humor, and self-transcendence. . . . Sex is the energy inside of us that works incessantly against our being alone.[6]

Sex and sexuality are God's gifts for us to enjoy, to be held together in our longings for pleasure and intimacy.

⚇ FOR CONVERSATION

1. How would you answer the journalist's question in the opening paragraph?
2. How do biological explanations of our sex drive and sexual bonding (see note 2) help you understand sexuality?
3. Which couple in the two stories in this reflection do you most identify with? In other words, to what extent are spirituality and sexuality joined for you?
4. What difference has it made—or do you think it would make—for you to hold sex, sexuality, and spirituality together?

EMBODIMENT

Steve

God created us as we are, embodied with flesh and blood and genitals. Therefore, we can embrace our bodies as good and enjoy them in healthy ways as a temple of God's Spirit (1 Corinthians 6:19).[7]

In Jesus—God's fullest revelation to us—"the Word became flesh" (John 1:14). Jesus had a body with genitals and (we assume) experienced sexual desire. When I was participating in a Men's Rites of Passage event in 2003 in a desert with other men, Richard Rohr stood in front of us with a large painting of the crucifixion. Jesus hung naked with his penis exposed. This startled me at first, but then I appreciated the bold display of Jesus in his humanity. Later when I brought a crucifix with a naked Jesus to church, our secretary reacted by saying, "We need to cover Jesus up" as she placed a sticky note on his genitals. This is what the medieval church did in the "fig leaf campaign" to cover up nudity in Renaissance art, like Michelangelo's naked *David* after it was unveiled.

Are we to be ashamed of our naked body and feel a need to cover up? Shall we have anti-body feelings long held by parts of the church? Do we need to react to an erection with "Bad dog, down!"? Or can we embrace our body as good, genitals and all?

Embodied as we are, consider the meaning of male genitals. Rohr suggests that our genitalia are metaphors for manhood:

> The male penis is both soft and hard. . . . There is a proper place for both in our lives, vulnerability and strength, letting go and firmness. Wisdom is to know when, where and how. The male penis is not a weapon or a mere tool, but a means of making contact, literally 'reaching out' for the other, not to hurt or to invade, but to pleasure and delight—mutually! It is the seed planter, the life giver, the enjoyer and the enjoyed.[8]

Rohr adds:

> Masculine energy is not just phallic but also scrotal. That most vulnerable, tender and protected part of a man—his testicles—are an essential symbol of his power and possibility. He carries a quiet, hidden seed. . . . His scrotum is a place of quiet ripening that must be protected and kept warm. It becomes power and pleasure when it comes forth. . . .
>
> An exaggerated phallic energy, uninformed by scrotal energy, is usually a sign of an intrusive, domineering and exploitive male. Your strong phallus

must always remember that it carries a soft sac of tenderness right beneath. The hard man without any softness is dangerous.[9]

Related to their penis, many men wonder, Is masturbation a problem? Anabaptist leader David Boshart offers this helpful response:

> Since the Bible is silent on the subject, the answer seems to be, "It all depends." Masturbation can easily become a compulsive behavior that becomes an end in itself. For some, masturbation is a way of avoiding intimacy. When a marriage falls on difficult times, masturbation can quickly become a way to remain distant. It can override the natural rhythms of sexual desire that motivate us to reengage our relationships with our spouses. . . .
>
> On the other hand, some masturbation may not carry such negative freight. In his book *Sex for Christians*, theologian Lewis Smedes says, "There are couples whose sexual needs come to a boiling point at very different temperatures; for a person whose boiling point is low, masturbation, rather than being a substitute for shared love, can be a safety valve." Another example might be those who once have known sexual fulfillment with a spouse but because of health or death cannot enjoy sex. Here, masturbation may be a way of lovingly remembering the love that was once intimately expressed.
>
> One thing is certain: Men masturbate. To answer their questions about masturbation, they need to end their silence and start talking about it.[10]

In addition to Boshart's comments, one might add that masturbation may be a healthy expression of physical embodiment and pleasure for people who are single or with partners who are not sexually intimate. Another "it depends" factor to consider is what may be used along with masturbation, like pornography, which objectifies others.

While some men easily joke about their genitals, others find it difficult to talk about. Consider having an honest conversation about the gifts and challenges of being embodied. As I shared in the introduction, once when my high school buddies joked about masturbating, I said that I did this. After a long pause, others said they did, too. This deepened our sharing and our friendship. After that conversation, I felt less alone and more at home in my body. And I think my friends did as well.

🗨 FOR CONVERSATION

1. What has helped or hindered your ability to embrace the gift of your body and sexuality?
2. When and how were sexual parts awakened in you?
3. How do you respond to Rohr's reflections on genitals?
4. When is masturbation a problem, and when is it okay?

EROS

Steve

Consider ancient verses from these erotic love poems:

His desire for her . . .

How fair and pleasant you are, O loved one, delectable maiden! You are stately as a palm tree, and your breasts are like its clusters. I said, "I will climb the palm tree and lay hold of its branches." O may your breasts be like clusters of the vine, and the scent of your breath like apples, and your kisses like the best wine that goes down smoothly, gliding over lips and teeth.

A garden locked is my sister, my bride, a garden locked, a fountain sealed. Your channel is an orchard of pomegranates with all choicest fruits.

Her desire for him . . .

Awake, O north wind, and come, O south wind! Blow upon my garden that its fragrance may be wafted abroad. Let my beloved come to his garden that he may eat its choicest fruits.

Invitation to the lovers . . .

Eat, O friends, and drink: drink deeply, O lovers!

Where are these from? The Song of Songs in the Bible.[11] The book is a bold display of erotic love and sexual passion that God created for a couple's intimate pleasure. The Song of Songs unveils this passion as a burning, erotic desire described as "flashes of fire" (8:6). It's written, "Many waters cannot quench love, neither can floods drown it" (8:7). The invitation is for the bride and groom to enjoy each other's bodies and be intoxicated with love!

For a healthy sexuality, we need to reclaim erotic love. While "erotic" for many refers to pornographic material and sexual things kept in secret, it means much more. The word *erotic* is based on the Greek word *erōs* for sensual love or desire for another person or for God.[12] C. S. Lewis describes eros as "being in love" and states that sexual desire without eros wants sex, whereas "Eros wants the Beloved."[13]

During a retreat on sexuality and spirituality, one man noticed how he had been too focused on "it" rather than "her." So, for sexual intimacy, instead of asking his wife, "Do you want to do *it*?" he'd like to ask, "Do you want to make love?"

To extend Martin Buber's expression, we desire an "I-thou" encounter more than an "I-it" activity. Another man mentioned that his question for his spouse is "Do you want to play?" as an invitation for good adult pleasure.

Recognizing the power of erotic desire, the Song of Songs provides this caution: "Do not stir up or awaken love until it is ready!" (8:4). Once aroused, erotic love is powerful and seeks a partner or an image. Lest we be overtaken by this passion and pulled into something inappropriate, we are called to practice self-control. For example, when Joseph was tempted by Potiphar's wife, he pulled away rather than being drawn into an adulterous union (Genesis 39). Commended for his self-control in 4 Maccabees 2, Joseph "overcame sexual desire" and "nullified . . . the frenzied urge of sexual desire" (2–4 RSV).[14]

Proverbs 5 conveys a wise warning to not be led astray but to fully enjoy the body of your spouse.

> Drink water from your own cistern,
>   flowing water from your own well.
> Should your springs be scattered abroad,
>   streams of water in the streets?
> Let them be for yourself alone,
>   and not for sharing with strangers.
> Let your fountain be blessed,
>   and rejoice in the wife of your youth,
> a lovely deer, a graceful doe.
>   May her breasts satisfy you at all times;
> may you be intoxicated always by her love.
>   Why should you be intoxicated . . . by another woman
> and embrace the bosom of an adulteress? (vv. 15–20)

> For an exercise, see **"Erotic Lovers in the Song of Songs"** at bit.ly/LivingThatMatters.

The call is for spouses to be "intoxicated" with erotic love for each other. What an invitation! And there's a call for self-control to rightly channel this gift of sexual passion.[15] While there is certainly a tension between these invitations, God wants us to enjoy the good pleasure of erotic love.

👥 FOR CONVERSATION

1. How do these reflections on eros compare to what you've been taught or have experienced about erotic desire?
2. If you are sexually active, to what extent do you focus on "doing it" (sex) versus "making love" when enjoying sexual passion?
3. What can our sexualized culture learn from the wisdom of these ancient perspectives on eros?

INTEGRITY

Steve

A common measure of a person's integrity is how they manage their sexuality.

As we aspire to be people of integrity, let's consider what integrity means, because it refers to more than just moral uprightness. The *Lexico* dictionary shows two meanings for *integrity*:

1. The quality of being honest and having strong moral principles; moral uprightness. Example: *She behaved with absolute integrity.*
2. The state of being whole and not divided. Example: *to respect the territorial integrity of the nation.*[16]

We often think of integrity in terms of the first meaning, believing it's about being morally upright and perfect. But who is perfect, especially when it comes to sexual issues? If, however, we focus on both meanings—being honest and having strong moral principles as well as being whole—then integrity is possible. It means being honest about how we fall short of our principles and how we fail to hold believing and behaving together.

Consider, for instance, how we split apart issues of sexuality with common divisions in dualistic thinking: splitting sex from sexuality, sexuality from spirituality, and body from spirit.

With these distinctions, we separate what belongs together. Generally, Hebrew faith with its more unified understandings of human life does not make such sharp divisions as Western dualistic thinking does. Sex and sexuality, sexuality and spirituality, body and spirit all belong together in an integrated whole. The older couple with their twin beds clamped together (see their story in "Sexuality" earlier in this section) practiced the truth of this wholeness.

For our sexual life, think of integrity as "getting our stuff together." This calls for us to examine our thoughts and actions, being honest with ourselves and others and pulling our divided parts together.

Reconsider another word that trips us up. In most translations we read in Matthew 5:48 that Jesus calls his followers to "be perfect" as God is perfect. What does he mean by this seemingly impossible command? If he means moral perfection, who can attain this? But Jesus isn't calling for "perfection" as we might think. Matthew uses the Greek word *teleios*—which means "complete" or "whole"—for what Jesus said. In other words, Jesus is calling for his followers to be made complete or whole. And *teleios* is related to *telos*, the word for "end" or "conclusion." Together, these two words suggest that we become complete or whole as we mature and reach our conclusion in following Jesus.

Understanding integrity in this way makes Jesus' call less a demand to be perfect and more an invitation to be whole. This feels less like a "should" and inspires more desire. With this understanding, there is also less shame when we fall short. And fall short we will, as we all struggle with one thing or another when it comes to our sexuality (the focus of our next topic).

Integrity also invites us to hold our unwanted parts together. Rather than cut off or cut out parts of ourselves that we don't like—our wounds, lusts, and difficult emotions—integrity recognizes that these are parts of our lives that have a crucial role to play in our wholeness if we will let them.

While we don't need to act on our unwanted parts or desires, neither do we need to fight them. We can simply acknowledge them and let them be while we listen for their deep wisdom, trusting God to bring about our wholeness. As Jesus said to his followers, "Let [the wheat and the weeds] grow together until the harvest," lest in pulling the weeds you uproot the wheat (Matthew 13:30).

> For an exercise, consider **"Sexual Integrity"** in the resources section.

🗎 FOR CONVERSATION

1. How does this view of integrity fit—or not—with your own experience?
2. What difference does it make for you to understand that Jesus calls us to wholeness, not perfection?
3. If you did the "Sexual Integrity" exercise in the resources section, what emerged for you?

CONFESSION

Steve

Sexual integrity is not easy. It calls for honesty, and honesty calls for confession—that is, telling the truth to God, to ourselves, and to others about how we struggle and fall short. This is hard, for it often involves a sense of shame or weakness.

When it comes to sexuality, we all struggle with one thing or another. As Richard Rohr observes in his book *From Wild Man to Wise Man*:

> Almost every man in western society suffers from some sexual wound. . . . I have never once had a man tell me that he felt his sexuality was whole, healthy and happy. It always seems to be a cross, a dilemma, a shame, a fear, a doubt or an impossible desire. Sexual issues are always at the heart of masculine spirituality. It must be tapped for good, or it will always be the "thorn in the flesh" that keeps men paralyzed, addicted and living double lives.[17]

Sexual wounds often lead to some form of struggle. The apostle Paul spoke of having a "thorn . . . in the flesh" (2 Corinthians 12:7). He also wrote about an agonizing internal conflict and being held captive by the power of sin:

> I do not understand my own actions. For I do not do what I want, but I do the very thing I hate. . . . For the desire to do the good lies close at hand, but not the ability. For I do not do the good I want, but the evil I do not want is what I do . . .
>
> So I find . . . that, when I want to do what is good, evil lies close at hand. For I delight in the law of God in my inmost self, but I see in my members another law at war with the law of my mind, making me captive to the law of sin that dwells in my members. . . . Wretched person that I am! (Romans 7:15–25)

Who can't identify with this?

We find consolation in Paul's words, realizing that we are not alone in our struggles. We don't know what Paul's thorn in the flesh or struggles were. But maybe that more easily allows his confessions speak to us.

Professor Keith Miller offers his own confession:

> When wrestling with a specific temptation, I seem to change into a different person inside. I have a kind of tunnel vision and only see the object of my resentment, greed, or lust. . . . Reason waits outside the door of temptation for me. I argue against my conscience and dazzle myself with agile rationalizations. By that time the battle is usually lost. . . .

There are long periods . . . when all the dragons appear to be dead. But then, one day when I am seemingly in good control of my emotions, I am suddenly in the midst of temptation. My senses are alive to the object of my resentment or my desire. I am practically engulfed in the urge to surrender to my inclination—to glorify my desires above everything—the instant they are born. And sweeping away reason, goodness, God's will, caution, and potential guilt—I succumb. . . .

Evidently in this life we will always have the occasional experience of succumbing to temptation. . . . The sad truth is that much of the time I am too weak to resist, and my failure is simply a hard, cold fact with which I must live. I have to come to God with the horribly uncomfortable feeling of failure. And finally, with no excuses, I force myself to my knees before Him in confession, asking for restoration . . . and self-acceptance by His grace. I thank Him that this process is what the gospel is about. . . . And asking Him for a new set of controlling desires, I thank Him for the miracle of forgiveness and the new start He can give me. I pull myself to my feet, brush the caked spiritual mud from my clothes and walk into another day as His child.[18]

While I seek to be a man of integrity, I admit to a history with pornography. Along with most men, I've struggled with pornography even though it violates everything I believe and value about honoring people and God's gift of sexuality. I identify with Paul's words about a perplexing, agonizing conflict within me. Feeling powerless and ashamed, I can say with Paul, "Wretched man that I am!" I have also experienced God's restoring grace that empowers recovery for sexual wholeness as I have shared about my struggles in my men's group. So I can also say with Paul, "Thanks be to God!"

For our integrity, confession about our "stuff" to our partners (if in an intimate relationship) and with others is essential. Vulnerability, sharing, and support are good for the soul and our growth. Men can practice these as we meet together, brother to brother, to bear each other's burdens and encourage one another so we may hold fast to living in love (Galatians 6:1–2; Hebrews 10:23–25).

> For more, refer to **"God's Gift of Sex and the Problem of Porn"** at bit.ly/LivingThatMatters.

 FOR CONVERSATION

1. What experiences have you had of confessing your struggles to others?
2. What makes confession so difficult that most of us carry our struggles alone in secret?
3. When you hear someone admit to a sexual struggle, how does this affect your view of this person?
4. What would be good for you to confess?

VISION

Steve

Who are we? Beloved children of God. And who are they, whomever they are? Beloved children of God. We are all beloved children of God created in the divine image.

This is how we are to see others and ourselves. This is critical, for how we look at others influences how we relate to them.

Parts of our culture, however, condition us to look at others as sexual objects.

For example, I am aware of how I, a straight man, may look at women. One time I noticed a woman walking in front of me wearing a top that exposed her bare shoulders. I was caught by a tattoo on her shoulder—*imago Dei*, Latin for "image of God." The tattoo invited me to look at who she is—a beloved daughter, created in God's image. Imagine what it would be like if all men saw others this way. There would be a lot more respect among the sexes and a lot more love in our relationships.

The truth of who we all are can correct our vision when it comes to how we look at and relate to others sexually. Jesus taught that our vision matters. He said, "The eye is the lamp of the body. So if your eye is healthy, your whole body will be full of light; but if your eye is unhealthy, your whole body will be full of darkness" (Matthew 6:22–23). He confronted how men looked at women, saying, "Everyone who looks at a woman with lust has already committed adultery with her in his heart" (Matthew 5:28).

How we act upon what we see can cause great harm. Consider King David when his eye became "unhealthy" in looking at Bathsheba as she bathed. Led by his lust and impaired vision, he abused his power and raped her (2 Samuel 11).

Our pornified culture takes this further with its objectification of women, men, and even children. Pornography distorts our vision by training our eyes to look at others as sexual objects for our lust rather than as human beings to respect. This violates both our own self and other people, degrades sexuality, and ruins sexual intimacy. As dehumanizing and damaging as it is, pornography is widely used and has a powerful hold on many people.

A more subtle and even more pervasive form of objectification takes place via "lookism"—seeing, valuing, and treating people based on their appearance. For females, clinical psychologist Mary Pipher states that this "poisoning culture" "limits [their] development, truncates their wholeness and leaves many of them traumatized," to say nothing about physical and sexual violations against them.[19]

Lookism affects not only the people we evaluate according to their physical appearance but also our own selves. Who of us has not measured our physical appearance against society's messages about what makes a person attractive? Which takes us right back to the starting block of understanding that we are all beloved children of God.

Taking Jesus seriously about how we look at others, let's consider a continuum with four levels of "looking" with regard to sexual intent:

1. Glancing: simple noticing
2. Looking: conscious observing
3. Staring: continued gazing
4. Lusting: sexual imagining

I can't help my glance in noticing those I find attractive, as this is something both instinctive and conditioned by our sexualized culture. I do have a choice, however, in how I look at someone. Will I stare, lust, or refocus my vision? Staring becomes a visual violation of privacy, and lusting leads to sexual objectification. Instead, I can refocus my attention to a person's face and look into their eyes to behold a beloved child and image of God. I can also focus my attention on seeing and valuing those I might not have noticed at first. "Overlooking" and "underlooking" are both ways of missing God's presence in another.

As Jesus taught, how we look at others matters. So pay attention to how you look at and relate to others. To refocus your vision, imagine an *imago Dei* tattoo imprinted on others. For this is who they are: the image of God. Consider what difference it makes to see others as a beloved child of God.

See also ***Seeking Sexual Integrity: Stories of Men and Pornography***, a downloadable PDF, under the JoinMen section of MennoniteMen.org.

For more, see **"Lust, Temptation, and Integrity"** and **"God's Gift of Sex and the Problem of Porn"** at bit.ly/LivingThatMatters.

 **FOR CONVERSATION**

1. What influences the way you look at others? And at yourself?
2. What do you notice about the way you look at others whom you find attractive? How does this affect how you relate to them? What do you notice about the ways you relate to those you find less attractive?
3. On the continuum of glancing, looking, staring, and lusting, where do you generally find your eye?
4. What helps you look at others with love and respect?

ORIENTATION

Steve

Same-sex orientation and relationships have been both a source of love and companionship and a source of pain and conflict.[20] As a pastor, I have listened to the joy of gay persons embracing who they are and having their same-sex union affirmed.[21] And I've heard the struggles of those who are, in the words of bridge-builder Justin Lee, "torn between being gay and being Christian."[22] One gay man in a men's group was so torn that he tragically ended his turmoil by suicide. In this same church, I also witnessed the joyous occasion of a gay couple blessed in a marriage ceremony. These moments represent a range of gay experiences in faith communities.

We need to understand that sexual orientation is not freely chosen, and it cannot be (or rarely has been) changed.[23] It's simply part of who we are. And our sexual wholeness requires that we embrace ourselves as we are and know that we are loved even though we may not fit certain norms. That we are intimately known and loved by God as expressed in Psalm 139:1–18 is true for everyone, no matter one's sexual orientation and gender identity—lesbian, gay, bisexual, cisgender, transgender, queer, heterosexual, asexual, nonbinary, and all others.

Sadly, the church, like much of society, makes it difficult for people whose sexual orientation doesn't fit the heterosexual box. In *Peaceful at Heart*, Pieter Niemeyer, a gay Mennonite, writes:

> The violence that has been perpetrated against the LGBTQ+ community, in the name of asserting masculinity, is why the "closet" exists for many [LGTBQ+] persons. A friend of mine shared that his father once sat him and his brothers down and said that if anyone of them were to come out gay, he would kill them. I asked my friend if he really believed his father would do such a thing, to which he responded that he absolutely had no doubt and that he therefore was in the closet for survival. Although this was not my reality, there was more than enough hostility in my life to realize the safety of the closet. . . .
>
> I knew God knew me at the deepest part of my being, and in God's love I never felt rejected—confused, yes, but never rejected. It was God's people that I worried more about.[24]

Describing the toll of life in the closet, Niemeyer adds:

As a gay man in the church, I had tried to live according to the traditional rules of masculinity and its intrinsic homophobia, thinking this was the right thing to do. Yet, to do this required living into both a profoundly discordant way of being and an ever-present sense of fear. If you are a straight cisgender (identify with the gender assigned to you at birth) person, imagine being told that you have to be in intimate relationship with someone of the same gender as you. I can well imagine it is a discordant way of imagining yourself. I can imagine that for many it is too much to ask. Closeted LGBTQ+ people navigate this way of living all the time within a predominant society that assumes heteronormativity. It is a physically, mentally, emotionally, and spiritually exhausting way of living.[25]

Gay people such as Niemeyer don't want to live alone exhausted in a closet. They want to live openly, freely, and safely. To love and be loved. To enjoy intimate relationships as heterosexual couples are able to. And to be fully affirmed and included in the life of the church. If our sexual orientation is a part of who we are and cannot be changed, can the church affirm and bless same-sex marriages so all people may enjoy such partnerships in life?

People answer this question differently, largely depending on their interpretation of scriptures. Some Christians with a traditional interpretation believe the Bible prohibits same-sex relationships. Other Christians believe that references to homosexuality do not relate to same-sex covenant unions today and that the Spirit is leading the church to be more inclusive, as in the case of the Jerusalem Council when the church discerned that certain biblical laws no longer applied in their situation (Acts 15:1–32).[26] People of faith have strong disagreements over this concern, just as people have had when interpreting the Bible on slavery, war, women in leadership, and divorce. No matter how we interpret the Bible on this question, scriptures clearly call us to forbear with one another in love and to "maintain the unity of the Spirit in the bond of peace" (Ephesians 4:3).[27]

God desires our wholeness, loves us unconditionally, and calls us to live in this love.

𓏢 FOR CONVERSATION

1. What is your experience with sexual orientation?
2. Of the experiences described in this reflection, what do you identify with or what have you seen?
3. What does it take for us to love ourselves and others as we are?
4. What are your perspectives about same-sex marriage?

IDENTITIES

Steve

Coming to terms with gender identity, along with sexual orientation, is essential for sexual wholeness. Gender isn't just about one's body. It's also about who we know ourselves to be. Having words to describe ourselves and our experience is helpful for understanding who we are as sexual beings. This is especially important when our gender identity does not necessarily match our sexual anatomy.

Being sensitive to gender identity is also important for relating to others. Some people simply dismiss this as "being PC"—that is, being politically correct. But rather than thinking about this as being politically correct, think about this as personal respect. How we think about ourselves and speak to others matters. This is especially true given the amount of fear, shame, and stigma surrounding sexual identity.

I think of a city judge in a congregation who made it his practice to show respect by asking individuals who came before his bench how they wanted to be identified, and then he addressed them in that way. By doing this, he wanted individuals to experience respect, not be misgendered, and receive equal protection. It was in this same congregation that I first encountered someone who identified not as "he" or "she" but as "they." This was difficult for some members in the congregation at first, since this didn't fit our social norms. Relating to this person as "they," however, not only showed respect but also helped them feel loved and a sense of belonging.

Understanding gender identities is difficult, and language around it can be confusing for many. This can be especially true for people brought up believing that there are just two biological options—male or female. In reality, not everyone fits neatly into these boxes.[28] We used to believe that biology encompassed only two kingdoms: plant and animal. A living thing was in one or the other. But fungi, for example, don't fit in either. Science now recognizes that there are not just two but five to eight kingdoms, depending on how one breaks down the categories. Take another example from biology. As sequential hermaphrodites, white mulberry (*Morus alba*) trees are gender fluid. They can be male or female or both, and can change their sex from year to year. Turns out living things are far more complex than once thought!

In *Peaceful at Heart*, Pieter Niemeyer describes how difficult it is for people who don't fit the norms:

I remember a kid from my school—on my bus route actually—who could not fit into those norms no matter how hard he tried. From an adult perspective, I now understand that this kid was transgender. If the traditional definition of being masculine is being non-feminine and eschewing anything in a man that might be considered feminine traits—however those are imagined—then transgender female children [male identified by birth, female identified by experience and expression] suffered mercilessly. In the face of their torment, I remembered feeling powerless, guilty, and very afraid. I felt that if I spoke up I would be "guilty by association" and subjected to the same treatment but, more than that, would be exposed. The school yard was the arena in which many of us LGBTQ+ children learned why it was essential to move into the closet. The closet is not something of our creation for the purposes of deception but is rather for our safety.[29]

Niemeyer points to how Jesus subverts certain norms and crosses boundaries in his encounter with the Samaritan woman:

She is a marginalized woman within a marginalized community, and he, a man, a teacher of Israel. The two were never supposed to cross paths, let alone encounter one another in such a profound way. It's a story that illustrates Jesus's abandonment of power, moving beyond binaries for the purposes of love. We are called to imitate such love.[30]

Regardless of whether we fully understand the complexity of gender identity, we do understand that God loves us all unconditionally and that we are to love as Jesus loved.

⚇ FOR CONVERSATION

1. What is your experience with gender identity?
2. Why does gender identity matter for sexual wholeness?
3. What does God's unconditional love and Jesus' example mean for the sexually marginalized?
4. How can we create safe, loving spaces for people to be who they are without shame and stigma? When have you experienced this kind of safety for yourself or others?

INTIMACY

Don

At the very end of the two creation stories in Genesis 1 and 2, a verse portrays the pure beauty and wonder of God's good work of creating humanity in the world. At the culmination of creation, Adam and Eve are described as "naked and . . . not ashamed." The suggestion here is that within the innocence and purity God intended is the freedom to be fully known and seen, without any need for hesitation or hiding or fear. This is true intimacy.

Psalm 139:1–2; 23–34 speaks of such intimacy with God:

O LORD, you have searched me and known me.
You know when I sit down and when I rise up;
    you discern my thoughts from far away. . . .

Search me, O God, and know my heart;
    test me and know my thoughts.
See if there is any wicked way in me,
    and lead me in the way everlasting.

God invites us into this space of welcome and being known and loved unconditionally—the way of ultimate peace!

Within our human relationships, our natural longing is to be fully known, seen, and received without judgment. This compels seeking after relationships that might offer this experience. The unfortunate reality is that many relationships fall short of healthy intimacy, and some folks, because of woundings in life, don't even know that intimacy is a goal to seek after. Too often, intimacy is equated with sexual encounters, the mechanics of which can be anything but intimate. Tragically, men often settle for only sex and never really know intimacy.

Meaningful intimacy involves vulnerability, mutuality, and respect. To enter into such a space with another person, we must feel safe enough to reveal ourselves at our deepest and fullest extent, even allowing ourselves to be drawn beyond what we might ever have known about ourselves. This may be achieved in moments in time with another, or over a series of many moments that make up a long and committed partnership. True intimacy involves our fullest selves and touches our souls.

The sharing of our physical selves in a sexual encounter can be an especially important and meaningful expression of intimacy. The wonder of God's creation has resulted in a high concentration of sensitive nerves that are in play when two persons move in sexual contact and rhythm. This includes our entire body's sensual responses and, in particular, our genitals. The reward centers of the brain and our highly developed hormonal system are triggered by the encounter, both responding to it and fueling the pursuit of pleasure. This may culminate in the climax of orgasm (which, contrary to socialization and modeling in movies, is not the be-all and end-all of intimacy). The resulting ecstatic experience of true sexual intimacy brings us as individuals into a close encounter with ourselves and with the other.

Intimacy, so highly valued and sought after, can also be a place of much pain when our vulnerabilities are used and abused by another who is seeking selfish gain. Exploitation of human longings for intimacy offers significant power to some, especially those who feel entitled to manipulate others without conscience. A huge industrial complex (e.g., advertising, pornography, music, and film) plays on the power of human sexuality to influence what we believe and what we consume. It ultimately wreaks havoc on our humanity, at both individual and corporate levels. That which has so much potential for beauty and healing also has potential for deep pain and destruction. Taking good care of our intimate selves and being careful with the vulnerabilities of others is essential.

In my many years of social work practice, I have heard countless tragic personal stories of those who have been victims of misuse and abuse of power that has led to intrusion into their most intimate ways of being. I have also journeyed with those who have abused, and been witness to their deeply wounded selves and the distorted thoughts and beliefs driving their hurtful behavior.

Our lives as intimately vulnerable people expose us to a wide range of experiences of beautiful, safe, and ecstatic connection with another as well as potential for deep pain. God help us nurture opportunities for wonder and protect us all from that which destroys!

⛉ FOR CONVERSATION

1. In what ways does society distort men's experiences of intimacy? How has this affected you or others you know?
2. How has your life been touched by intimate connections with others?
3. In what ways do we have responsibility to and for each other to protect and nurture healthy vulnerability?
4. What helps and hinders your experience of intimacy?

FIDELITY

Don

In the context of sexual wholeness, fidelity means expressing oneself sexually in a committed relationship with only one other person. Within the Christian tradition, sexual intercourse—the most intimate and vulnerable we can be with our lover in a bodily sense—has historically been affirmed exclusively in the context of a marital commitment between a man and a woman.[31] Engaging in genital intercourse with someone outside of marriage has traditionally been considered crossing over a clear line into infidelity.

As we broaden our understandings of sexuality and as the nature of relationships has changed dramatically in our society, defining fidelity has become much more nuanced and challenging. The blurring of boundaries around sexual expression—by agreement between partners, as in polyamorous relationships, or through betrayal of covenant—has rarely been as pervasive and blatant as we experience in society today. We are recognizing more than ever before that a wide array of behaviors can undermine our sense of safety in relationship. Our ability to be vulnerable with a partner depends on our understanding of their commitments to our well-being and to the relationship itself.

The forms of partnered relationships are remarkably varied and include, among others, traditional heterosexual marriages, same-sex marriages, unmarried partnerships, and nonsexual partnerships.

Society has often given men greater liberty—generally unspoken—to be sexually active outside of marriage. With the assumption that "this is just how men are," society has not generally punished such behavior. "Line-crossing" behavior has simply been expected and often supported by peers who have pretended not to notice, or have even intentionally aided the behavior.

What does scripture have to say about fidelity? Sexual themes pop up frequently within the pages of the Bible. Numerous passages describe the infidelity of Israel to God in the Old Testament (Exodus 32; Hosea 5) and of humanity to God in the New Testament, in parables for example (Mark 12:1–8). The words *faithfulness* and *unfaithfulness* commonly carry similar meanings to fidelity and infidelity. When Jesus, in his Sermon on the Mount, highlights the warning against adultery in the Ten Commandments, he does so to broaden the Law's understanding of sexual infidelity to include looking at a woman "with lust" (Matthew 5:27–28). In essence, he says, "Your definition of sexual infidelity is too small! Adultery begins as you give in to the temptation of crossing sexual boundaries in your inner world."

Jesus calls us to recognize that both our imaginations and our actions are included under the realm of fidelity. We cannot avoid our natural wiring being triggered by sexual images that surround us, but we definitely can choose whether we turn toward or away from such images and the temptations that build over time.

Part of the challenge of such choice is that our society bombards us with varying messages about fidelity and faithfulness. A whole industry designed to blur or totally erase the limits pressures us from every angle, forcing us to choose daily what kind of men we will be.[32] Will we take second glances at attractive bodies? Consume pornography? Cross sexual boundaries with someone other than our spouse?

If we give in to such behaviors, shame often accompanies our actions. To complicate matters, we have amazing capacities to justify our actions—no matter how small—falsely minimizing the impact of our choices. Ironically, this increases the likelihood of continuing such behaviors, which can then take on compulsive qualities if not addressed.[33]

Though our fidelity choices are personal, the journey does not need to be a solitary one. Establishing a relationship of accountability with a trusted friend is one way to strengthen our resolve to live faithfully into our preferred self as a beloved child of God.

Sexual integrity and fidelity are some of the most challenging aspects of life that men face. You are not alone. Peace to you!

FOR CONVERSATION

1. How has the phrase "That's just how men are" affected you, others you know, or situations you are aware of? Is this phrase still relevant today?
2. How has male power and privilege contributed to the lack of fidelity in our society?
3. In this time of changing sexual norms, what can society and the Christian church learn from each other about fidelity?
4. How would you describe your "preferred self" in terms of sexual fidelity?

As section 4 ends, let's stop to notice what's happening with us. After a minute of silence, discuss:

- How are we experiencing our open conversations?
- What gifts, difficulties, or tensions do we notice?
- Where is God's Spirit at work within and among us?

Social Practices

INTRODUCTION

Steve

> *You shall love your neighbor as yourself.*
> **—Jesus, Mark 12:31**

THIS SECTION IDENTIFIES social practices. While these topics could be called "values," we claim them as practices to emphasize that we hold them not simply as important ideals but also as essential practices that we live out.

Together, these practices aim to establish shalom so that God's will is done on earth as it is in heaven. *Shalom* is the rich Hebrew word for a peaceable order with abundance, security, and justice for all and well-being throughout creation. In the subtitle of his book *Shalom*, Perry Yoder states that shalom is "the Bible's word for salvation, justice, and peace." He writes, "It points positively to things being as they should be. . . . Only a transformation of society so that things really are all right will make for biblical peace."[1]

In these topics, we refer to social problems, like sexism, racism, injustice, where things are not right. As described in the introduction to this handbook, we approach social problems from within a positive framework. More than just condemning what we're against, we describe what we're for. Take sexism, for instance. Rather than focusing on dismantling patriarchy, we call for action to create respect, equity, and justice for women. In doing constructive work, we seek to cast a vision of God's shalom with its values and practices to move us to change. As the appreciative inquiry model shows, what we focus on becomes our reality, and since focusing on problems may amplify them, we instead focus our actions on bringing about shalom. As we do this, we call forth positive change, which, in turn, transforms problems.[2]

We focus on the following social practices:

Respect. Holding another as valued through our words or actions builds human relationships. Receiving genuine respect from another can be life-giving.

Compassion. Jesus called his followers to be compassionate as God is compassionate. As we see in Jesus' life, compassion recognizes what others experience, helps us empathize with them, and moves us to action to address personal and social needs.

Inclusion. Certain people traditionally have been (and some still are) excluded because of one or more of the following: skin color, religious beliefs, income, gender, sexual orientation, physical ability, political opinions, appearance. The Gospels describe how Jesus responded to social exclusion and modeled the way of loving inclusion for all people as God's beloved children.

Mutuality. The numerous "one another" phrases in the Bible envision a world of relationships where respect and compassion are practiced and received freely, where shared responsibility for the other is the basis of healthy relationships and community.

Freedom. Freedom is a value of great regard, and we are challenged by the implications that our freedoms may be at the expense of the freedoms of others. God's gift of freedom comes at the expense of the freedom not to love, because love is ultimately meaningful only when it is freely offered.

Equity. We continue to struggle with human tendencies to place differing values on people and to enforce inequities. Jesus models the biblical call to end divisions and hierarchies.

Justice. No justice, no peace, the biblical prophets would proclaim today. God's shalom requires social justice as the social expression of God's love. Justice is what love looks like in public.[3]

Diversity. Against cultural supremacy, we are to embrace diversity, believing that all people are beloved children of God created in the divine image. While we recognize the existence of the social construct of race—and the harms caused by racism—we also uphold that there is only one race: the human race, with rich expressions of manifold differences.

Sustainability. The garden of Eden represents what God intended: beauty, biodiversity, and abundance. We're to care for the earth and live in sustainable ways so that God's abundant life of shalom is enjoyed by all from generation to generation.

Love. The thread that energizes and informs all these social practices is the experience of God's love for us, received in healing and humility and then offered forward in both personal and social expression.

Empowered by the Spirit, we carry out these practices with a vision of God's shalom on earth as it is in heaven.

For supplementary materials and exercises, see what's provided in the resources section and at bit.ly/LivingThatMatters.

RESPECT

Don

Respect has often been a significant concept within masculine culture and roles, carrying different meanings in different contexts.

Traditionally, respect has had a flavor of hierarchy and loyalty, as possibly reflected in 1 Peter 2:17 (KJV): "Honour all men. Love the brotherhood. Fear God. Honour the king." Respect, or honor, has been considered something to be gained or lost through one's actions—possibly on the battlefield or through an act of bravery—or granted via one's social class or position.

Respect has also been demanded from others through threats, with disrespect commonly prompting a response of force. In the movie *The Godfather: Part II*, older brother Fredo is passed over by his own father in the succession of power. Struggling to find his place in the world, he demands "I want respect" from his younger brother Michael Corleone, "the Godfather," who ultimately delivers the chilling judgment, "You're nothing to me now."

While these forms of respect maintain a certain "order" in society, they clearly do not align with our Christian understandings of mutual humility and love (Matthew 20:26; John 13:34; Romans 12:10).[4] This is especially the case when respect is forced as a tool of the powerful to systematically disadvantage others.

Might there be another understanding of respect that enhances life and relationships? Dictionary definitions of respect speak of "esteem," "deep admiration," "understanding," and "due regard" for the other. When joined with Christian values of humility and love, respect does indeed contribute to healthy human existence, both in the giving and in the receiving of it.

When we truly respect someone, they receive messages of affirmation and value that lead to their growth and thriving. And we are not humiliated or diminished in the process. When we receive such messages of respect from others, we are encouraged along our way, and we rise to the opportunity to live up to this honoring. When respect is received from someone who is acting with authenticity and kindness, it builds and strengthens the best of who we are and can become.

I have observed in my counseling practice that people who are disrespectful of others are generally motivated by beliefs and values that consider those others to be inferior. In such cases, a person's comments reflect prejudices and stereotypes that place the other below them—sometimes explicitly, often in subtle ways. What is often apparent as well is that the need to diminish another person comes from deep places of insecurity.

Disrespect diminishes both giver and receiver. Conversely, respect gives life. Treating a client with genuine respect allows their insecurities to diminish. This enables them to be fully present to the process of change and to face their life with honesty.

> For more, consider **"A Time of Reckoning for Men and Masculinity"** and **"Men's Work"** at bit.ly/LivingThatMatters.

 FOR CONVERSATION

1. In what ways do men use respect as a tool of destructive behavior? As a tool of positive behavior?
2. When have you experienced (or witnessed) giving or receiving respect based on actions, social class, position, or threat?
3. When have you received or given respect that included humility and love? What was that like for you?

COMPASSION

Steve

Once upon a time, two brothers farmed together. They shared equally in all the work and split the profits evenly. Each had his own barn. One of the brothers was married and had a large family; the other was single and lived alone. One day the single brother thought to himself, "It's not fair that we divide the grain evenly. My brother has many mouths to feed while I have but one. I know what I'll do. I will take a sack of grain from my barn each night and put it in my brother's barn." So each night after dark, he carried a sack of grain to his brother's barn.

Now, the married brother thought to himself, "It's not fair that we divide the grain evenly. I have many children to care for me in my old age, and my brother has none. I know what I'll do. I will take a sack of grain from my barn each night and put it in his barn." And he did.

Each morning the two brothers were amazed to discover that though they had removed a sack of grain the night before, they had just as many. One night the two brothers met each other halfway between their barns, each carrying a sack of grain. Then they understood the mystery. And they embraced, loving each other deeply.

A Jewish legend says that God looked down from heaven, saw these two brothers embracing each other in compassion, and said, "I declare this to be a holy place, for here I have witnessed extraordinary compassion." It is also said that on this spot Solomon built the first temple.[5]

It's almost magical what compassion can do. Where it happens is holy and transforming.

Compassion is core to Christian life. It's a divine characteristic that embodies God's presence in human experience, especially in suffering, and it brings about healing change. The word *compassion* comes from the Latin words *com* and *pati*, which together mean "to suffer with." The supreme example of this is God becoming incarnate in the person of Jesus, or Emmanuel—which means "God with us." And what do we see with Jesus? One who was present to people in their pain or need and responded with acts of transforming love.

Jesus called his followers to be compassionate as God is compassionate (Luke 6:36). As we see in the life of Jesus, compassion recognizes what others experience, helps us empathize with them, and moves us to action. As an expression of love, compassion moves us to address personal and social needs. With compassion, we see need, feel pain, and act.

Henri Nouwen writes:

> Compassion asks us to go where it hurts, to enter into places of pain, to share in brokenness, fear, confusion, and anguish. Compassion challenges us to cry out with those in misery, to mourn with those who are lonely, to weep with those in tears. Compassion requires us to be weak with the weak, vulnerable with the vulnerable, and powerless with the powerless. Compassion means full immersion in the condition of being human.[6]

Compassion is not simply empathy or being sentimental. It also involves action to bring about change so people may experience the abundant life God intends for all to enjoy. As Nouwen states:

> Honest, direct confrontation is a true expression of compassion. . . . We cannot suffer with the poor when we are unwilling to confront those persons and systems that cause poverty. We cannot set the captives free when we do not want to confront those who carry the keys. We cannot profess our solidarity with those who are oppressed when we are unwilling to confront the oppressor. Compassion without confrontation fades quickly into fruitless sentimental commiseration.[7]

 FOR CONVERSATION

1. When have you shown compassion to others? What difference did it make?
2. When have you received compassion? What was this like?
3. How have you seen compassion transform relationships?
4. Where have you witnessed compassion with confrontation for social change?

INCLUSION

Steve

In the classic story *Animal Farm*, barnyard animals revolt and set out to establish a better social order than what they had under the farmer. After the revolution, they create commandments to reorder their life: No human is above them. No one calls another "Master." All animals are equal and included in their life together. But in the course of time, pigs take charge and arrange things to their benefit. With their power, pigs reduce the commandments from seven to one: "All animals are equal, but some animals are more equal than others."[8] Certain animals regarded as "lower animals" are not allowed to partake of the prosperity of Animal Farm. In their second-class position outside the house, those animals watch pigs inside enjoying what they are denied.

George Orwell based this "fairy story" on his observations of human behavior in social orders. He drives home the point that no matter what a group or constitution may say, "some are more equal than others." Societies may claim otherwise even while treating some as less equal and deserving while giving power, privilege, and goods to others.

Wherever the animal farm or human group may be, some people tend to be treated as second-class citizens, denied certain benefits and excluded from opportunities that others have. Individuals and entire groups are not allowed to fully participate in the economic, social, and political life of their society based on skin color, religious beliefs, income, gender, sexual orientation, physical ability, intellectual ability, political opinions, or appearance.

This also happened in the time of Jesus. The Gospels describe Jesus modeling the way of loving inclusion for all people as God's beloved children in his responses to the following types of social exclusion:

- *Class-based exclusion*—when Jesus called working-class fisherman as his disciples and future church leaders
- *Gender-based exclusion*—when Jesus developed close relationships with women and drew them into his circle of disciples
- *Ethnic-based exclusion*—when Jesus extended healing to the Syrophoenician's daughter and the centurion's servant
- *"Purity"-based exclusion*—when Jesus made physical contact with individuals considered unclean

- *Conduct-based exclusion*—when Jesus let in women engaged in prostitution and became known as a "friend of sinners"
- *Age-based exclusion*—when Jesus called to himself children who were kept aside
- *Party-based exclusion*—when Jesus invited both Matthew as a tax collector (supporting Rome) and Simon as a Zealot (resisting Rome) into his circle

Jesus' interactions with two socially excluded outsiders—a Samaritan woman and a Syrophoenician woman—are especially interesting. When Jesus relates to the Samaritan woman at the well, he crosses boundaries between men and women, Jews and Samaritans, religious and sinners. The woman is surprised by his inclusive actions (John 4:1–30). By contrast, Jesus appears to mistreat the Syrophoenician woman because of her ethnic identity. To his surprise, she confronts his exclusive healing. He then extends God's healing to her daughter as requested (Mark 7:24–30). This Syrophoenician woman had something to teach Jesus!

Having observed Jesus' response to outsiders, Paul proclaimed that Jesus had broken down dividing walls to create in himself one new humanity in place of two (Ephesians 2:14–15). Based on both our common identity as God's children and what God had accomplished in Christ, Paul wrote that there are no longer distinctions like Jew or Gentile, slave or free, male and female (Galatians 3:28). Extending the way of his brother Jesus, James confronted class-based distinctions practiced even in Christian community (James 2:1–6).

Unlike the banquet at the end of Animal Farm, where only pigs feed at the table while other animals watch from outside, the great banquet that Jesus describes includes "the poor, the crippled, the blind, and the lame" and people off the street (Luke 14:15–24). No one is more equal than others. Everyone belongs and fully participates in the community. All are inside together and enjoy God's abundant life. This is God's shalom.

FOR CONVERSATION

1. How have you experienced exclusion or inclusion, and how has this affected you?
2. Who are marginalized people groups in your community? Who's kept outside or from the table?
3. What will it take to include them as full participants of your community?
4. What do you do to include marginalized people in your life? What difference does this make for them and for you?

MUTUALITY

Don

An often-repeated term in the Bible is "one another." The following lengthy list of how we are to treat one another paints a picture of what mutuality means: we are to be devoted, show honor, live in harmony, build up, be like-minded, accept, admonish, greet, care for, serve, bear with, bear burdens, forgive, be patient, speak the truth, be kind and compassionate, submit to, comfort, encourage, exhort, stir up, show hospitality, pray for, confess to, and—ultimately—love one another.[9] In short, we are to have reciprocal relationships not qualified by rank, position, or merit.

God calls us to practice mutuality in our dealings with others—an ideal that may seem too big for us to reach. And that is exactly why we must rely on God's Spirit (1 Corinthians 12:7) to work in us as we open ourselves in humility and grace. Jesus, in the Sermon on the Mount, shares a similar instruction: "In everything do to others as you would have them do to you; for this is the Law and the Prophets" (Matthew 7:12). The assumption in this "golden rule" is that mutuality is the path to true and right relationships. Reciprocity—the mutual exchange of goodwill and action—is life-giving for us as human beings.

In a world characterized more by animosity and suspicion than mutuality, where men often feel responsible to serve as "protectors," it may be difficult for us to embrace an ethic of mutuality. We find it challenging to rise above our defensive impulses and seek relationships of cooperation and interdependence. Men have also generally been socialized to be aloof and hold a position of power over others, both of which work against healthy mutuality. Although giving up this posture of patriarchal privilege in order to give and receive in true mutuality will feel vulnerable, it's the way of life-giving love. And the working of God's Spirit within us is calling us to this way.

Healthy mutuality offers safety and welcome. If we experience the "one another" list not only as something we do for others but also as something we receive from others, we may be surprised and intrigued by the possibilities of such loving-kindness. Mutuality recognizes that both parties in a relationship benefit from the interchange. Men, though silently longing for and craving such welcome and safety, sometimes do not see themselves as deserving such treatment, or they fear it might make them soft.[10] It is a tragic loss for all when we are unable to open ourselves to this powerful human experience.

This kind of mutuality doesn't just happen; it requires us to lean into it by choice. This is especially true if you have been schooled in the kind of masculinity that tells men to "be strong, not weak"; be the head of the household; and operate from a position of aloofness, power over others, and control.

In my practice, I have seen many men struggle with the challenge of shifting away from a position of entitlement toward mutuality with others. Male entitlement runs deep from role models in our lives and from beliefs promoted by culture or religion. For some men, the discomfort of having these basic values challenged is so strong that they choose to discontinue counseling. For other men who are able to open themselves to others with humility, treating them with equality and respect, the opportunities are great.

Mutuality is a path of healing and growth that brings us more fully into alignment with God's calling to live well with one another. It's a powerful opportunity for new freedom and joy. Let's venture in!

 FOR CONVERSATION

1. What relationships of mutuality have you experienced?
2. Do you long for or hesitate to enter such relationships—or both?
3. What keeps you from enjoying relationships of mutuality in your life?
4. How might the practice of mutuality transform you and relationships in your life?

FREEDOM

Don

Freedom is a value held in high regard by people around the world. The democratic West in particular claims to have a corner on creating freedom for the people within its borders. When we move beyond the ideal to the reality of our lives, however, the discussion becomes more complex as we realize that freedom is relative. Our view of freedom will be shaped by where we are located on the continuums of power (e.g., specific to race, gender, economic status). That's because the cost of freedom can be very different from group to group.

We cannot simply claim freedom without questioning the costs to all involved—especially when freedom is claimed by the more powerful, who selectively offer it with clearly defined limits to the marginalized. For example, what are the costs of freedom in the history of North America for Indigenous people and for those descended from people who were enslaved?

Freedom generally defined is "the power or right to act, speak, or think as one wants."[11] Similarly, social freedom is the condition that allows people to go about their lives and interact free of oppression and coercion, with the ability to live according to their own beliefs, values, and intentions. For example, we in North America live relatively free to practice our religious beliefs. We are also increasingly free to pursue relationships without religious or state-sponsored determinations of which relationships are morally right or wrong for us.

Where freedom, even relative freedom, is ours, we have the corresponding responsibility to live well, to the fullest of God's good will for us. Christian values of love, justice, and mutuality open our eyes to also recognize that our freedom is not true freedom when it is at the expense of others' freedoms or well-being.

The question is often asked, Why would God grant freedom to humans when it results in such destruction, evil, chaos, and pain? In situations of confusion, pain, and fear, some would counter this question by stating, "God is in charge." The tension between these positions leaves many of us bewildered. Ultimately, I find it hard to believe we are simply marionettes in some cosmic puppet show. Any image of a divine being orchestrating the minute details of our lives, including the most gruesome and tragic, paints a horrible picture of God. I would need to question whether such a God is deserving of our worship.[12]

Dallas Willard states in *The Divine Conspiracy*, "God has paid an awful price to arrange for human self-determination."[13] Such self-determination, he suggests, is the only way God can experience the kind of personal, free beings whom God desires to be in relationship with. Love cannot be compelled—whether toward God, human beings, or creation. True love must be accompanied by the freedom not to love, or it is not love!

So freedom, even with its tragic possibilities, is ultimately an invitation. God offers us healing and release—freedom from the constraints on our ability to love ourselves and others. And God provides us with a calling and the Spirit's presence—freedom for the life we were created to live in communion with God, with creation, and with one another.

FOR CONVERSATION

1. In what ways do you see freedom used destructively? In what ways do you see it used toward healing?
2. What does freedom as an invitation to love God and others mean to you?
3. How would you describe your image of God? What does this God have to say about human freedom and divine will?
4. How does your personal freedom affect the well-being of others?
5. How do you (or how would you like to) practice freedom as part of God's shalom? What is the importance of this practice for you and others?

EQUITY

Don

Two thousand years ago, Paul made a radical declaration about Jesus' good news: "There is no longer Jew or Greek, there is no longer slave or free, there is no longer male and female; for all of you are one in Christ Jesus" (Galatians 3:28). This was a boat-rocking statement of truth at that time, and it continues to challenge the world today.

Posturing for power and seeing "the other" as a threat to our interests continues to create hierarchy, division, and destruction.[14] Historical forces, often rooted in religious belief systems, have classified people by characteristics including gender and skin color. This has created inequitable systems based on patriarchal values and assumptions that have generally benefited white men and disadvantaged women, girls, and minorities.

As a result, white people—primarily white men—have assumed power and control over others. They have done so both directly through physical or sexual violence, for example, and indirectly through manipulating financial, legal, or educational systems. And they have often done so with a sense of entitlement and impunity.[15]

Achieving equity (equal outcomes) means more than treating individuals equally. Equity is reached by distributing resources and opportunity according to need. In too many areas of society, inequity between different groups of people has become status quo—just the way things are. If you benefit from the inequities, this kind of systemic inequity can be hard to see, even if you are fair-minded and well-meaning.

Righting historical inequity in social systems demands intentional rebalancing. This often means siding with those who are disadvantaged and speaking strongly against injustice (Isaiah 1:17; Matthew 25:40; Micah 6:8). This must be a goal that we strive to meet daily both at a societal level and with individuals.

The work of equity calls for humility and sacrifice. It first requires honest self-evaluation, and sometimes the help of others, to see the spaces of inequity in our lives. We can then move from awareness to action. Breaking down barriers to equity requires actively loving one's neighbor (Mark 12:31) and even loving one's enemies (Matthew 5:44).

Jesus himself breeched historical hierarchies in how he related to women and minorities. His conversation with the woman at the well, for instance, crossed significant gender and racial norms (John 4:4–27). We cannot ignore this radical picture of Jesus healing divisions during his earthly ministry. Our call is to follow Jesus into similar acts of tearing down walls of separation and injustice.

The Christian church has been on both ends of the spectrum—sometimes struggling to consistently live and witness to this call and other times helping individuals and communities move toward practices of greater equity. In my thirty years as a social worker, for instance, I have witnessed devastating abuses of power, primarily by men toward women and children. The rigidly held beliefs and values of some men about the place of women have resulted in violence and oppression experienced by women. On the other hand, I have also witnessed the possibility of change when healthy, safe relationships are developed with men who have abused others. Such relationships can open the door for men to share their stories and can challenge their core beliefs about both equality and equity.

> Refer to **"Women in the Bible"** at bit.ly/ LivingThatMatters to understand the biblical basis for liberation from patriarchal control.

FOR CONVERSATION

1. In what ways do you benefit from power and privilege? In what ways might you feel disadvantaged?
2. In what ways do you see the church being (or having been historically) part of the problem of inequity? In what ways do you see the church actively working toward equity?
3. How have you experienced the cultural shifts of the past half century that have exposed male privilege?
4. How does Jesus' example of relating to the Samaritan women of his day challenge us to live the truth of Galatians 3:28 today ("No longer Jew or Greek, slave or free, male and female . . .")?

JUSTICE

Steve

"No justice, no peace!" rings the chant raised in response to racial injustice. Political protestors didn't make this phrase up; biblical prophets did. Jeremiah railed against those who spoke "peace, peace" when there was no peace (6:14). While there may not have been war at the time of Jeremiah, there were injustices and oppression. So, with no justice, no peace.

The prophet Amos was especially forceful in opposing poverty and oppression. He called on God's people to "hate evil and love good, and establish justice" (Amos 5:15). He confronted the complacent in their worship while they neglected God's call for justice. "Take away from me the noise of your songs; I will not listen to the melody of your harps. But let justice roll down like waters, and righteousness like an ever-flowing stream" (5:23–24). Micah asks, "What does the LORD require of you but to do justice and to love kindness and to walk humbly with your God?" (6:8).

Recall God's purpose to establish shalom in the world—a peaceable order with collective abundance, security, and justice for all. As Noel Moules states, like a threefold intertwined cord, God's shalom requires

- Physical and material well-being and dignity for all things
- That every relationship is just and right
- That each person has spiritual integrity and uprightness in character[16]

The Hebrew word *tzedakah* can be translated as either "righteousness" or "justice."[17] This reveals the necessary connection between right relationships and social justice in the eyes of God. No *tzedakah*, no *shalom*. No justice, no peace.

When Jesus announced his mission in Luke 4:18–19, he quoted the prophetic vision of God's justice in Isaiah 61:1–2 and spoke not only of personal healing but also of social justice (Matthew 23:23). In ministry as a shalom activist, Jesus went about the work of establishing God's justice, especially with women, the poor, and other marginalized people. What injustices would Jesus confront today to seek God's peace?

- Patriarchy, sexism, racism, and gender inequality
- The rich getting richer while the poor get poorer
- Oppression and violence against people of color

- The displacement of Indigenous peoples from their land
- Mass housing of people in prisons
- Inhumane treatment of immigrants
- Environmental degradation and its impacts
- The system of white supremacy and privilege[18]
- Any case of inequality, exclusion, or oppression

What Jesus would do we must do, for we are not only his followers but also his body. As Teresa of Ávila said, "Christ has no body now but yours, no hands, no feet on earth but yours. Yours are the eyes through which he looks compassion on this world. Yours are the feet with which he walks to do good."

We must speak and act for justice. We cannot remain silent. Nor can we be neutral. South African archbishop Desmond Tutu observed, "If you are neutral in situations of injustice, you have chosen the side of the oppressor. If an elephant has its foot on the tail of a mouse, and you say that you are neutral, the mouse will not appreciate your neutrality."[19] Or as philosopher Elie Wiesel said, "We must take sides. Neutrality helps the oppressor, never the victim. Silence encourages the tormentor, never the tormented. Sometimes we must interfere."[20]

Justice is the social expression of God's love. Professor Cornel West put it best: "Justice is what love looks like in public." Or as professor Omid Safi says, "Justice is love, embodied."[21] The justice-making of US congressman John Lewis illustrates what love looks like in public.

In Lewis's last appeal to action for peace with justice days before his death, he drew upon his lifelong struggle for justice and the teachings of Rev. Dr. Martin Luther King Jr. We are all complicit, he wrote, when we tolerate injustice. "Each of us has a moral obligation to stand up, speak up and speak out. When you see something that is not right, you must say something. You must do something." Sometimes this means "getting in good trouble, necessary trouble." His final published words were: "So I say to you, walk with the wind, brothers and sisters, and let the spirit of peace and the power of everlasting love be your guide."[22]

> For more on God's call for peace with justice, see our book ***Peaceful at Heart: Anabaptist Reflections on Healthy Masculinity***.[23]

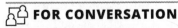 **FOR CONVERSATION**

1. What injustices capture your attention and why?
2. How have you experienced or been a part of injustice?
3. How have you been engaged in working for justice?
4. What does justice-making require of you?

DIVERSITY

Steve

Many in my community were shocked when the Ku Klux Klan came to Goshen, Indiana, not once but twice in the late 1990s with their hateful ideology to target people of color.

In response, local high school students worked with city leaders to create and post colorful "Embracing Diversity" signs at the entrances to our community. As a counter-demonstration to the KKK rally, many people gathered for a "celebration of diversity" event to enjoy a rich variety of foods, music, dance, and presentations. This became an annual event to witness to what our community stands for. Since that time, we have publicly acknowledged our shameful past of being a "sundown town"—excluding people of color from living in town. While the community is becoming increasingly diverse, we still have work to do to fully embrace diversity, dismantle racist structures, and achieve God's shalom for all people.

In many ways, our community is a microcosm of a historical culture of white supremacy built on the notion that white men and their ideas and ways are superior to people of color and their ideas and ways. Most of us don't like to admit this. After all, we've opposed the Klan, put up signs, and made statements declaring what we stand for. Nevertheless, remnants of the larger system remain intact, preventing full expression of diversity and justice.[24]

White supremacy culture allows groups and nations to act in ways contrary to what they claim to espouse. As author Robin DiAngelo observes,

> The United States was founded on the principle that all people are created equal. Yet the nation began with the attempted genocide of Indigenous people and the theft of their land. American wealth was built on the labor of kidnapped and enslaved Africans and their descendants. Women were denied the right to vote until 1920, and black women [and men, practically speaking,] were denied access to that right until 1964.[25]

Theologian Walter Brueggemann points out that we're dealing not just with white supremacy but also with white Christian superiority when it comes to people of other faiths. This is deeply rooted in the Doctrine of Discovery, when the church legitimized white, Western European control over Indigenous peoples.

> It is clear that "the other"—non-Christian, nonwhite, non-Westerner—does not need to be honored if and when Christian white Westerners are in all cases and

circumstances superior. The entire trajectory of superiority serves to diminish and dismiss "the other" as an important and defining presence in the world.[26]

Brueggemann traces this problem through history as it relates to Israel, the church, the United States, and white people, and how they saw themselves as chosen. He concludes that chosenness is immensely problematic as it leads to entitlement, exclusion, displacement, and domination. "This chosenness . . . takes on an ideological force that is unquestioned in its legitimacy and, for the most part, unrestrained in its practice."[27]

We reject white supremacy and Christian superiority as an ideology and must dismantle it as a system. All people are God's beloved children created in the divine image, regardless of color, culture, or creed.[28] This is a fundamental truth that points to the dignity and equality of all people and paves the way for the right ordering of society. We cannot deny the harms committed because of the human construct of race. We do not support false ideas of "colorblindness" or "not seeing race." But we do assert that in God's creation, there is only one race—the human race, with rich expressions of manifold differences.

Diversity is part of God's design for humanity, as we see in the many tribes and nations in Genesis. Yes, Israel was "chosen." But it was set apart, not set above other peoples. It was chosen to be a people of God and a blessing to all families of the earth (Genesis 12:1–3). This went awry when chosenness turned into cultural supremacy that gave way to entitlement, exclusion, and domination (also seen today in Palestine). Even in Jesus' interaction with the Syrophoenician woman (Mark 7:24–30), we see a disturbing expression of Jewish superiority.

In the story of Pentecost (Acts 2), we witness the amazing event of God's Spirit falling on people who had significant cultural differences. Amid their new spiritual unity, great social diversity remained. Then in Revelation we have a vision of "a great multitude . . . from every nation, from all tribes and peoples and languages" standing together before God (7:9). Here's the ultimate celebration of diversity—the whole human race together with all its differences, likely at a heavenly banquet with wonderful foods, dancing, and music.

👥 FOR CONVERSATION

1. What would our life be like without diversity?
2. What are the gifts of diversity? The challenges?
3. How have differences in race, ethnicity, gender, and faith enriched your life or community?
4. In what ways have you experienced people trying to suppress differences and limit the embrace of diversity? Why do you think they do so?

SUSTAINABILITY

Steve

In the beginning, God created the planet and provided ample resources for the life of all its plants and creatures. Rich soil, clean water, clear air, and more—all in a life-giving balance. The garden of Eden represents what its Creator intended: beauty, biodiversity, and abundance. We're to care for the earth and live in such a way that God's abundant life of shalom is enjoyed by all from generation to generation.

Environmental sustainability is central to our stewardship of the earth. By sustainability we mean meeting the needs of the present without compromising the ability of future generations to meet their needs.[29] Sustainability is about upholding and leaving things in a state that's as good as or better than when we received them. In ancient Athens, city leaders took an oath to "leave the city, not less but greater, more beautiful and prosperous" than it was left to them.[30] Imagine what the world would be like if all its leaders and people lived by this oath not only with their city but also for all the earth!

We need to care for the earth's resources, being mindful of the larger community. Certain Native American traditions teach that we must consider the impact of our actions for the next seven generations. As one elder advised, "You must not think of yourself or of your family, not even of your generation. . . . Make your decisions on behalf of the Seven Generations coming, so that they may enjoy what you have today."[31]

God cares for not only the human community but also the biodiversity of the entire planet. For God desires the well-being of all the earth's ecosystems, where all resources, plants, and animals (including humans) exist in a life-giving balance. When people live as if they are all that matters, this balance is compromised.

Take trees, for example. Remove too many and the balance is upset. As a word, *sustainability* was first used in 1713, where it meant to never harvest more trees than what the forest could produce in new growth. Tragically, this has not been practiced. Since humans began clearing land and logging, the number of trees on earth has fallen by 46 percent.[32] And in just the past thirty years, the world has lost 440 million acres of forest.[33]

Cutting too many trees has severely compromised this most important means of capturing carbon and cooling the planet. Now, with global warming, climate change threatens life on the entire planet. The world is already suffering the extinction of animal and plant species, food loss, forest fires, floods, droughts, and expanding deserts. The United Nations reports that "the health of ecosystems on which we and all other species depend is deteriorating more rapidly than ever . . . [, affecting] the very foundations of our economies, livelihoods, food security, health and quality of life worldwide."[34] And the worst is yet to come unless we change our ways and restore the earth.

We need to face and change how much we consume of the world's resources. If everyone lived like the average North Americans, we would need four planets![35] This is not only unjust but also unsustainable. And in the words of theologian and activist Randy Woodley, "When something is unsustainable, you can be sure it will eventually come to its end."[36] We all need to consume less so we can love our neighbors (of all species), the earth, and future generations.

The triple bottom line model (see figure) provides an integrated approach to sustainability. This model includes three interrelated spheres: people (society), profit (economy), and planet (environment). With all this in mind, we ask:

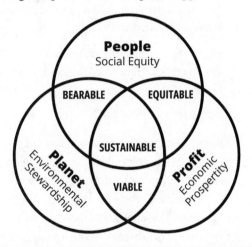

- Is our level of consuming the earth's limited resources equitable, viable, and bearable?
- Are we leaving our planet not worse off but better for the generations to come?

For an exercise, calculate what you consume and your ecological footprint using the online inventory at FootprintCalculator.org.[37]

To participate in our campaign to plant one million trees to help restore the earth, check out JoinTrees at MennoniteMen.org.

To live more sustainably, see **"Caring for the Earth"** at bit.ly/LivingThatMatters.

🗣 FOR CONVERSATION

In what ways do you practice sustainability in how you live your life?

1. If you took the online ecological footprint test, how many planets would it take if everyone else consumed as much as you?
2. What are ways you can reduce your footprint and live more sustainably to preserve God's shalom?

LOVE

Don

It would not be a leap to suggest that all of what we are working toward in this handbook is grounded in our understanding of love. Indeed, God's calling and intentions for humanity are all framed in the Bible by the primacy of love!

> You shall love the Lord your God with all your heart and with all your soul and with all your mind and with all your strength. . . . You shall love your neighbor as yourself. (Mark 12:30–31)

> And now faith, hope, and love remain, these three; and the greatest of these is love. (1 Corinthians 13:13)

> This is my commandment, that you love one another as I have loved you. No one has greater love than this, to lay down one's life for one's friends. (John 15:12–13)

> God is love. (1 John 4:8)

Books, podcasts, and sermons have tried to describe and inspire love. Movies and songs have explored the dimensions of love in many forms. Greeting cards and memes try to boil it down to a few words and images. And yet love continues to be elusive or fleeting for many. At our basic levels of existence, we long to be loved—unconditionally. We thrive in an atmosphere of love, and we can literally die because of an absence of the loving care of others. The tragic outcomes of the absence of love in life are pervasive in our world.

Some stereotyped images of men elevate the ideal that real men need no one (i.e., do not need to experience the love of another person). Other stereotypes suggest that men express and experience love primarily through only one body part. The truth is that healthy masculinity flourishes when we fully embrace all of our humanity. It is in giving and receiving love that we are fully alive, as intended in God's good design.

The full embrace of giving and receiving love requires two of the more difficult practices that are discussed in the Personal Challenges section of this book—empathy and vulnerability. Both of these practices present chal-lenges for many of us because strong messages and socialization have failed to affirm and nurture these skills in men. Also, some men experience trauma in their lives that results in a compulsive need to armor up against further pain. These men can then feel overwhelmed by exposure to meaningful, loving relationships.[38]

Men will do well to consider how self-understandings of masculinity or a history of trauma can restrict both giving and receiving love. As I sometimes say to clients, "It's really tough to make love in knight's armor . . . lots of clanging around but very little meaningful connection!" Healing opportunities and the pursuit of practices of self-discovery and openness can free us so that we can more fully experience this beautiful and life-enhancing gift from our creator God![39]

Love also functions at social levels. For example, the organization Mennonite Disaster Service provides opportunities for participants to love their neighbors by sharing time, skills, and resources to respond to disasters in North America. In the summer of 2019, MDS collaborated with Woodland Community Centre of Brantford, Ontario, in a special arrangement to assist with renovating the former Mohawk Institute Residential School.[40] The school had been part of a more-than-140-year cultural disaster perpetrated against Indigenous people in Canada in the nineteenth and twentieth centuries. In light of this history, a very important part of the collaborative effort included survivors from the school sharing with MDS participants about how colonial history has harmed Indigenous people. Creating such space to hear each other's stories opens doors for love to step in and restore our common humanity.

The transforming power of God's love flowing through us into the world brings about God's shalom, God's good will for creation. Each act, individually and collectively, contributes to the healing work of the Spirit as we work toward mutuality and respect, loving all creation compassionately.

FOR CONVERSATION

1. How has your upbringing restricted or enhanced your ability to receive and give love?
2. How have experiences of trauma—as a child, in relationships, or in employment situations (first responders, crisis workers, employment accidents)—inhibited your ability to receive and give love freely?
3. How has the love of others been life-giving for you?
4. When have you witnessed love bringing positive change to social problems in your community?
5. In what ways can you extend love in your community beyond personal relationships?

As section 5 ends, let's stop to notice what's happening with us. After a minute of silence, discuss:

- How are we experiencing our open conversations?
- What gifts, difficulties, or tensions do we notice?
- Where is God's Spirit at work within and among us?

Conflict Tools

In This Section

Conflict

Power

Postures

Nonviolence

Courage

Self-Control

Listening

Speaking

Responses

Collaboration

INTRODUCTION

Steve

Let everyone be quick to listen, slow to speak, slow to anger.
—James 1:19

WE DON'T HAVE TO LOOK FAR to realize that life is full of conflict. It's in our families, intimate relationships, and friendships. And we see it in the community and across our nations. We must learn to respond to conflict in constructive ways lest our differences divide us and break our relationships. In *The Naked Anabaptist*, Stuart Murray states: "As followers of Jesus in a divided and violent world, we are committed to finding nonviolent alternatives and to learning how to make peace between individuals, within and among churches, in society, and between nations."[1]

This section focuses on tools for transforming interpersonal conflicts. In the first session, we claim that conflict is normal and natural in our relationships. While conflict can be destructive, it also can bring growth or change. We can embrace conflict as an opportunity to deepen relationships, bring about new growth, mobilize constructive energies, and witness the power of creative love. To learn how to make peace with conflict, we examine directives and examples we find in the New Testament.

We then examine power, which is always involved in conflict: we define power, identify what gives us power, and describe how it can be used and abused. We recognize how men have too often used power for their benefit against those with less power. God calls us to use our power to correct what stands against love and to establish God's justice.

Next, we address three postures in conflict: aggressive, submissive, and assertive. Following the way of Jesus, we renounce acting in aggressive ways. We also question the traditional submissiveness often taught in the Anabaptist tradition. Instead, we uphold assertive responses in conflict, believing this is the "third way" of Jesus.

From the stance of assertiveness, we turn to nonviolence and how to respond when conflict turns violent. We address the difficult question often put to people committed to peace: What would you do if someone physically assaulted you or a loved one? In response, we discuss how assertive, nonviolent force may be used as we reinterpret Jesus' teaching in Matthew 5.

Next, we look at two emotional reactions in conflict that can get us into trouble: fear and anger. Out of fear, we can easily give in or give up in conflict or give way to aggression. We may be anxious about how someone will react to us or may be afraid of getting hurt. When fear overtakes us, it's hard to stand up or speak up and engage others in conflict. For moments like these, we need courage. If we react out of anger, we run the risk of escalating the conflict and acting with aggression. To manage this difficult emotion, we discuss ways of practicing self-control.

We then consider listening and speaking in conflict, starting with the counsel of James: "Let everyone be quick to listen, slow to speak, slow to anger" (1:19). Careful listening can go a long way to defuse tension and create understanding. We then discuss speaking skills and offer the models of centered speaking and nonviolent communication for verbal assertiveness.

Next, we examine five responses to conflict: (1) accommodate, (2) compromise, (3) avoid, (4) compel, (5) collaborate. Which of these styles a person uses tends to depend on their level of concern both for goals and for relationships in a given conflict. We describe each of these styles, along with their pros and cons, and name an online inventory to identify your own conflict response tendencies.

Finally, we focus on collaboration—that is, working together with others to transform conflicts. For this, we offer the Peacemakers stoplight model for collaborative problem-solving. The lights signal us to stop to see the problem, think how to resolve it, and act in a way to make peace with conflict.

Supplemental exercises and additional material are provided in the resources section and at bit.ly/LivingThatMatters

Mennonite Men also provides a retreat and workshops on making peace with conflict for groups or congregations interested in interactive sessions on learning practical skills for transforming conflict.

CONFLICT

Steve

Life is full of conflict. Consider conflicts in our families, intimate relationships, and friendships. Witness conflicts in the community and across your nation. Think of conflicts in churches. In over thirty years of pastoral ministry in seven churches, I have had a front-row seat to many conflicts. Pick an issue: politics, the president or prime minister, capital punishment, abortion, climate change, war, hell, same-sex unions, immigration, and more. We have our differences, and our differences too often divide us. That Western society socializes us to think in terms of win-lose and strong-weak often makes conflict more difficult.

In this section we focus on interpersonal conflict, which we define as a problem between at least two interacting parties who perceive incompatible goals. In short, it's simply a problem between people.

Before reading on, stop here and complete the "How I Experience Conflict" inventory in the resources section. After completing the inventory, ask yourself what stands out to you about your experience with conflict. As I've listened to hundreds of people report their responses to it, I've noticed that adverse metaphors, difficult feelings, and negative assumptions far outweigh positive ones. It's no wonder so many of us struggle with conflict.

What we believe about conflict influences how we feel and respond to it. If we believe conflict is bad, we will likely have negative feelings about it and try to avoid or suppress it. If, however, we reframe conflict as an opportunity for growth or change, we can embrace it.

All of us experience conflict. It's simply part of life and relationships. Conflict is neither good nor bad. It simply is. Created as we are with differences, conflict is inevitable. The concern is not whether we have conflict but how we respond to it. Depending on our response, conflict can be either destructive or constructive. If handled well, conflict can deepen relationships, bring about new growth, mobilize constructive energies, establish new identity, energize relational life, and release the power of creative love.

The Bible is full of conflict. Look at Cain and Abel (Genesis 4:1–16), the family of Israel (Genesis 37–50), the circle of Jesus' disciples (Luke 9:46), the early churches (Acts 6:1–6; 15:1–7; 1 Corinthians 1:10–11), and many other biblical relationships. Many people, even mature adults like Paul and Barnabas, sometimes respond to conflict poorly and end up in broken relationships (Act 15:36–40).

Jesus calls us to make peace with conflict, and to deal directly with those involved (Matthew 5:23–24; 18:15). If this approach does not resolve the conflict, then others may intervene as advocates or mediators to help bring resolution (Matthew 18:16–18).

Jesus said that God's Spirit guides us to redemptive and constructive responses to conflict (Matthew 18:9–20). Conflict can be an opportunity for growth and change, even fresh revelations from God. We see this in the council in Jerusalem when they addressed a major conflict over whether male Gentile Christians, as members of the Christian community, could keep their foreskins (Acts 15:6–29). The gathered group realized that this conflict was more than skin deep; it had to do with welcoming cultural differences in the Christian community. In this instance, people of faith with contentious differences worked together in the Spirit to discern a new revelation from God that opened the faith community to be more inclusive. Here's a case where a difficult conflict became an occasion for something good, especially for men with foreskins!

Aware that reactions to conflict can break relationships or hurt people, Jesus and Paul called for restoration (1 Corinthians 7:10–11), healing of hostilities, and renewal of relationships (Matthew 5:24; Ephesians 2:11–20). Paul told us to forbear with one another in love, making every effort to maintain the unity of the Spirit in the bond of peace (Ephesians 4:1–6). This becomes possible as we learn to be accepting of others, forbearing of differences, patient in spirit, ready to forgive, humble, and loving (John 13:34–35; Ephesians 2:14–16; 4:1–3; Colossians 3:12–16).

Our differences can divide us, but they don't have to. A close pastor friend and I differ from each other on many political and religious issues. We have been at opposite ends of the continuum on difficult issues. And yet we love and respect each other as brothers. Our friendship transcends our differences, and we find that we learn and grow from our conflicts. As Proverbs 27:17 puts it, "Iron sharpens iron, and one person sharpens the wits of another."

Embrace the opportunity to make peace with conflict.

> For an exercise, complete the inventory **"How I Experience Conflict"** in the resources section and check out **"The Anatomy of Conflict"** at bit.ly/LivingThatMatters.

🗣 FOR CONVERSATION

1. What did you notice in completing the conflict inventory?
2. What's difficult about conflict in your experience?
3. How has what you've learned about being a man influenced how you respond to conflict?
4. When has conflict brought about something good for you, and what did it take for that to happen?

POWER

Steve

Men are socialized to seek and use power. I admit that I feel more like a man when I'm running my large chain saw, hauling a load of logs, operating my skid steer, competing in a martial arts tournament, or shooting my .308 hunting rifle.

What all these activities have in common is the exercise of power. While men often think about power in relation to equipment, skill, and physical strength, power is much broader than this. Power is the capacity to be and do or make something happen. It's the ability to accomplish or influence an outcome.

What gives us power? Our age, gender, race, education, ability, appearance, intelligence, sexual orientation, vocation, nationality, religion, income, personality, and social connections.

Individuals with a lot of power are often unaware of their power, the ways they express it, and how they benefit from power in their life. They can easily misuse their power and harm others in the process. Those with much less power may feel ashamed, controlled, frustrated, angry, hopeless, or helpless.

Beyond personal power lies systemic power. This is the power within cultural patterns and institutions that allows one group to impose its standards, goals, and norms on another group. Individuals and groups with social power often don't recognize this, or may even deny it.[2] But systemic power is real and operates all around us, privileging, for example, men over women (patriarchy) and white people over people of color (racism and white supremacy).[3]

Power is involved in all conflict. Like conflict, power is neither good nor bad. It simply is. It's how we use it that matters. In relation to self or others, consider ways we use power:

- Power *within*—claiming our identity and dignity
- Power *to*—exercising our agency to shape our lives
- Power *for*—serving the needs or interests of others
- Power *with*—joining others to achieve some good
- Power *over*—dominating or controlling others
- Power *against*—violating the well-being of others[4]

In conflict, it's important to be aware of how we're using our power, especially when there's an imbalance of it. It's too easy for those with greater power to misuse it for their benefit at the expense of those with lesser power. Men taught to take charge, dominate, or be in control, for example, are set up to use power over and against rather than with and for others. Such men often feel entitled to use their power as they want.

Martin Luther King Jr. said, "There is nothing wrong with power if power is used correctly." Power and love are not opposites as often thought, where "love is identified with a resignation of power, and power with a denial of love." Instead, "what is needed is a realization that power without love is reckless and abusive, and love without power is sentimental and anemic. Power at its best is love implementing the demands of justice, and justice at its best is power correcting everything that stands against love."[5]

God calls us to use our power to correct what stands against love and to establish God's justice. We are called to follow the example of Jesus, who was the most powerful man on earth. He used his power not to advance or benefit himself but with and for others to serve their well-being out of love. He made it clear to his disciples when they sought a position of power that his way was not to lord over others but to serve them (Matthew 20:28). Paul invites us to have the same mind of Jesus, who did not exploit power but used it to serve the interests of others (Philippians 2:3–7).[6]

In *Peaceful at Heart*, David Evans states,

> I am learning that the power of love can inspire my imagination to conceive of new ways to relate to others. Instead of dominating, I can defer to the wisdom of others. Instead of controlling, I can collaborate with others. Instead of struggling stoically through life, I can express the full range of my human emotions. Only the power of love could liberate me from the prison manpower constructed, and that is a lesson men must share for generations to come.[7]

> For an exercise, see **"Power Sculpture"** at bit.ly/LivingThatMatters.

FOR CONVERSATION

1. What sources of power do you have in your life?
2. How do you use your power in conflicts at home, work, and church and in the community?
3. What's it like for you to use your power with and for others? When have others used their power with and for you?
4. In what ways do you sometimes use your power over or against others? In what ways have others used their power over and against you?
5. What have you been taught as a male to do with power?

POSTURES

Steve

When facing a conflict where you feel emotionally attacked or physically threatened, how do you respond?

In such a situation, people usually choose one of three basic postures: submissive, aggressive, or assertive.

Submissive or aggressive. Based on our fight-or-flight instinctive reactions to threat, we are naturally submissive or aggressive.[8]

Submissive	Aggressive
Cower	Threaten
Bow down	Strike back
Capitulate	Retaliate

To diagram these stances between other (O) and self (S), consider this figure:

Self submits;	Self is aggressive
other prevails over self.	in order to prevail over other.

In our dominant culture, men are taught to be aggressive in defending themselves in conflict or when threatened. To "be a man" means to stand your ground, be tough, and defend yourself, even if that means being violent. It's a matter of taking control and staying on top. This response often escalates rather than transforms conflict.

By contrast, men in the Anabaptist peace church tradition have most often been taught to be submissive and "turn the other cheek." This is based on a certain interpretation of what Jesus says in Matthew 5:38–39: "You have heard that it was said, 'An eye for an eye and a tooth for a tooth.' But I say to you, Do not resist an evildoer. But if anyone strikes you on the right cheek, turn the other also." It's important to note that the Greek word Jesus uses here for resist—*antistenai*—means "violent resistance." So this is better translated "Do not violently resist . . ."

Assertive. Following the biblical work of Walter Wink, I believe we have often misinterpreted Jesus.[9] While Jesus calls for nonviolence, he does not teach nonresistance. Rather than being submissive or aggressive, Jesus teaches and models being assertive. This is the "third way" of responding to conflict—through non-violent assertive action to transform conflict and violence (which we'll look at next in the "Nonviolence" reflection).[10]

Instead of one person being on top and prevailing over the other, in being assertive (from the Latin *asserere*, "to join") we act in ways to join the other side by side to transform conflict and potential violence.

In a diagram, the assertive stance looks like this:

Act in ways to join others for the well-being of both self and other.

In our Making Peace with Conflict retreat, I invite two men to reenact the scene in *The Adventures of Robin Hood* when Robin Hood and Little John first meet and end up fighting over who's going to cross a narrow bridge first. I give the participants foam bats to role-play this fight on the "bridge," and then we discuss the problems with fighting—like risking injury and escalating violence. They also role-play submissive options and discuss how these can enable the continuation of disrespect or abuse. Then I ask the whole group of men to discover alternatives to being submissive or aggressive. When they look for a third way, they come up with many assertive options to resolve the conflict.

The finest of these is one where Robin Hood and Little John join hands, help each other pivot on the bridge, and go on their way with a win-win resolution.

Desmond Tutu, the archbishop of Cape Town, faced this situation for real. It happened in the time of apartheid in South Africa when people of color were oppressed and had to give way to Afrikaners and other white colonizers. Tutu, a Black bishop in the church and spokesperson against apartheid, was walking by a construction site on a temporary sidewalk the width of one person. He was at the beginning of the sidewalk when a white Afrikaner appeared at the other end and recognized Tutu, saying, "So it's you, Bishop Tutu. I don't make way for gorillas." In response, Bishop Tutu stepped aside, made a sweeping gesture, and said, "Ah, yes, but I do." With wit and wisdom, Tutu demonstrated an assertive response to aggression. And so can we.

FOR CONVERSATION

1. How would you describe your natural stance in conflict when emotionally attacked or physically threatened?
2. When does your stance change and why?
3. In what ways would you like to grow in your response to conflict?
4. What is your understanding of the way of Jesus for responding to conflict, and how does this compare to what you were taught as a man?

NONVIOLENCE

Steve

Jesus said, "Love your enemy." Gandhi taught, "An eye for an eye makes the whole world blind." And Martin Luther King Jr. said, "Returning violence for violence multiplies violence." We hold these truths for the way of peace.

But when conflict turns violent, how shall we respond? What would you do if someone physically assaulted you? Or a loved one, as Goshen College professor James Miller faced in 2011 when someone brutally attacked his spouse Linda in their home? How do you reconcile your responses with the nonviolent way of Jesus?

In the previous reflection, we looked at three basic postures in response to conflict that feels threatening. Rather than being submissive or aggressive when emotionally attacked or physically threatened, there's a third way—being assertive. When it comes to violence, Anabaptist Christians believe that Jesus calls us to practice nonviolence. This is not submissive nonresistance but assertive nonviolence, which seeks to prevent violence and to act for the well-being of all involved.

In our Making Peace with Conflict men's retreat, we play out all three of these responses to violence in several exercises:

- *Submissive.* In one exercise, an aggressor forcefully grabs our wrist and pulls us against our will. In a submissive response, we don't resist, and the aggressor continues to violate us. With this, we get a taste of what it's like to have our space violated, be controlled by another person, and feel powerless.
- *Aggressive.* By contrast, I demonstrate an aggressive response with a controlled elbow blow to the face of the aggressor as he pulls me toward himself. Many men say I have a right to do this and that the aggressor had it coming. But I don't think this counter-aggression is the way of Jesus.
- *Assertive.* So we turn to an assertive response with an aikido wrist escape. With this, we move to the side of the aggressor, turn, and simply lift our arm in a way that easily breaks his grip. This leaves us free of his control and standing by his side to look together for another way to resolve the problem. We don't move against the aggressor but simply move in a way that disables his attack. This follows the teaching of Sensei Morihei Ueshiba, the founder of aikido, who taught, "Protect the attacker, for to control aggression without injury is the art of peace."

As I write in an article about martial arts as a model for nonviolence, we have alternatives to being submissive or aggressive.[11] We can be assertive (again, from the Latin *asserere*, "to join") to join the aggressor and act for their well-being and that of everyone involved in the violence. While being submissive can give tacit support to violence and being aggressive can provoke greater violence, being assertive is more likely to overcome violence as it demonstrates a respect for each person involved. Assertive action can include the use of force—psychological, social, or physical—to stop violence and protect all involved, including aggressors.

On one occasion, I used nonviolent physical force when someone who was high on cocaine attacked my wife Linda. To stop this person from harming her, I took them down to the floor and restrained them in a control hold until the police (another form of force) arrived. This was physical force used only to prevent violence. It harmed no one.

Based on Jesus' teachings in Matthew 5:38–42, the "third way" of nonviolence can be described in these terms:

- Assert your own humanity and dignity as a person.
- Stand your ground and seize the moral initiative.
- Find a creative alternative to violence.
- Break the cycle of humiliation.
- Expose the violence or injustice of the other or system.
- Surprise others with actions for which they're unprepared.
- Be willing to suffer rather than retaliate.
- Cause the other to see you in a new light.
- Deprive the other of responses where force is effective.
- Seek the other's transformation and well-being.[12]

This is a nonviolent way of peace. One that is neither submissive nor aggressive but active and assertive.

> For more, see **"The Biblical Call to Nonviolence and Peace"** at bit.ly/LivingThatMatters.

FOR CONVERSATION

1. How have you been taught to respond when conflict turns violent?
2. What would you do if someone physically assaulted you or a loved one?
3. How do you reconcile your response with the nonviolent way of Jesus?
4. What do you think about using nonviolent physical force to control another person's aggression?

COURAGE

Steve

Two difficult emotions in conflict—fear and anger—can get us into trouble. To transform conflict, we must learn how to manage these emotions within ourselves.

We'll begin with fear. (Anger is our next topic.) With fear, we can easily give in or give up in conflict or give way to aggression. We may be anxious about how someone will react to us or may be afraid of getting hurt.

When fear overtakes us, it's hard to stand up or speak up and engage others in conflict. For moments like these, we need courage. (Of course, when fear signals real danger, we need to pay attention to it, not "be a man" and react with foolish, daring behavior.)

Courage is not the absence of fear. It's the strength to face and overcome fear. Nelson Mandela modeled such courage when he confronted apartheid in South Africa. He was continually threatened and eventually imprisoned for his stand against systemic racism in his country. After his release from prison, he went on to become president of South Africa. He won the Nobel Peace Prize for his bold, courageous work for human rights, racial equality, and multiracial government. He wrote,

> It is from these comrades in the struggle that I learned the meaning of courage. . . . I have seen men and women risk and give their lives for an idea. I have seen men stand up to attacks and torture without breaking, showing a strength and resiliency that defies the imagination. I learned that courage was not the absence of fear, but the triumph over it. . . . The brave [person] is not [the one] who does not feel afraid, but [the one] who conquers that fear.[13]

In Montgomery, Alabama, Rosa Parks overcame her fear with courage as she engaged in her historic act of civil disobedience. In violation of racial segregation laws at the time, she refused, as a Black woman, to give up her bus seat to a white man—an event that helped initiate the civil rights movement. Regarding what it took to engage race-based conflict, she wrote, "I have learned . . . that when one's mind is made up, this diminishes fear; knowing what must be done does away with fear."[14]

Closer to home, I recall the story that JoAnne Lingle shared in a sermon about how her work of peacemaking also began on a bus seat. At the age of ten, she was the only white person riding on a bus through an African American community in Savannah, Georgia. The bus began to fill up with other riders until no seats were left except for JoAnne's bench seat. According to Jim Crow racial segregation laws, a person of color could not sit with her. Observing an elderly Black woman with a cane step onto the bus, JoAnne shared,

> I watched her as she tried to stand and keep from falling. I could no longer watch! I jumped up to give my seat to her. The driver stopped the bus and said to me in a stern voice, "Little girl, sit down! Don't ever give your seat to a [racial slur]!" Having been taught to always obey authority, I sat down and cried all the way home. Where were the grownups who would speak for justice? Where were they who were unafraid to do what was right?

Later in life, JoAnne recalled this incident and refused to stay seated or remain silent. She joined Christian (now Community) Peacemaker Teams, and to this day, she confronts injustice, oppression, and violence in the United States and around the world. She refers to her nonviolent civil disobedience as "divine obedience," saying, "I believe the only things that are really mine are my voice and my body. They are mine to give for others, as Jesus gave his to me."[15]

When God's people faced the invading king of Assyria, they were terrified. King Hezekiah, who "did what was good and right and faithful before the LORD his God," said to the people, "Be strong and of good courage. Do not be afraid or dismayed before the king of Assyria. . . . With him is an arm of flesh; but with us is the LORD God, to help us and to fight our battles" (2 Chronicles 31:20; 32:7–8). Then and throughout the course of history, people of faith have found strength to overcome fear and stand firm in God. And so can we.

We can recall words like these as well as human examples to help us face our fears in the strength of God. One practice to help manage fear is centering. For this, take slow, deep breaths—breathing in through the nose and out through the mouth—to relax your body and pay attention to the wisdom within you. Along with this, you might want to focus on a word, phrase, scripture, or image to help center yourself.[16]

This practice allows the Spirit within us to make us strong, loving, and wise in our responses.

FOR CONVERSATION

1. What makes you anxious or afraid? What do you fear in conflict?
2. When you experience fear, what happens in your body or mind that impairs your ability to respond?
3. How do you face and overcome fear in your life?
4. What experience might you share of being empowered to act when facing something threatening?
5. Traditional masculinity believes men shouldn't feel fear. How does this belief affect you? How might it prompt foolish reactions in the face of danger?

SELF-CONTROL

Steve

In addition to fear, another emotion to manage in conflict is anger. We feel anger in reaction to threat, injustice, and underlying feelings of fear, pain, loss, or harm. In this sense, anger is a gateway emotion that can lead us to the true causes of our emotional upset if we take the time to uncover them. Because of how we are socialized as men, we often default to anger and fail to tune in to more core emotions. This may mean missing important opportunities to name and address these other emotions. This is more likely for men than women since men are often given more permission to act out their anger.[17]

Anger comes from a Latin word meaning "to strangle"—which anger can feel like and lead to! *Anger* is only one letter short of *danger*; we need self-control lest our conflict escalates and we strangle someone! As Proverbs 15:18 says, "Those who are hot-tempered stir up strife, but those who are slow to anger calm contention."

Anger is common in conflict. Like conflict, anger is neither good nor bad. It just is. What matters is what we do with anger. Paul says, "Be angry but do not sin" (Ephesians 4:26). If we frequently feel angry, however, there may be something in our life that needs attention.[18]

Anger and other emotions simply are what they are. It is difficult, if not impossible, to control our emotions. Rather than attempting to do so, we can recognize them, listen to them to understand what they are about, and be wise in how we respond. While we may not be able to control our experience of anger, we can control our reactions. Notice how quickly we can control our anger when we politely answer the phone! We can do the same when answering conflict.

We have three basic choices for handling our anger when in conflict:

- *stuff it*, risking depression or resentment;
- *act out*, reacting with aggression to hurt others;
- *direct it*, focusing its energy to transform conflict.

(D)anger: Raw anger stuffed down or acted out can lead to the following:

- *resentment* (hateful anger toward others);
- *rage* (consuming anger that burns within us);
- *retaliation* (vengeful anger to strike or strangle).

Consider what one man learned after he reacted with raw anger and became violent. From prison, he wrote:

> The single toughest, most dangerous opponent I'd ever faced—the one that truly hurt me the most, causing me to spend 30 years of my life behind bars—was my own anger and fear. I write these words now, a gray-haired old man, hoping to God—before you suffer what I've suffered—that it will cause you to listen and learn Nonviolent Communication. It will teach you to recognize anger before it becomes violence, and how to understand, deal with, and take control of the rage you may feel.[19]

Whereas raw anger that's acted upon may harm, processed anger can

- alert us about something that needs our attention;
- prevent us from simply giving in to conflict;
- energize us to respond with intention, putting passion into action.

For example, when Jesus was angry and drove out the money changers in the temple, he put his anger into action to stop people from using the temple as a marketplace (John 2:13–17).

Here are seven "Rs" for what we can do with our anger in conflict:

- *Refrain* from reacting impulsively out of raw anger by taking a timeout.[20]
- *Relax* by taking slow, deep breaths with centering (described in the previous reflection, "Courage").[21]
- *Reflect* on emotions underlying our anger.
- *Retrieve* the message that anger conveys.[22]
- *Reframe* troubling thoughts that are triggering our anger.
- *Release* unreasonable demands or expectations.
- *Redirect* processed anger into assertive action.[23]

As we know from our experience, anger can be an overpowering emotion and can lead to harm. However, we have options for tending and managing our anger in healthy ways for something good.

🖧 FOR CONVERSATION

1. What do you tend to do when you're angry?
2. What impact does your anger have on others? Ask persons close to you how your anger affects them.
3. What helps you practice self-control, calm down, and channel your anger?
4. When has processed anger led to something good for you or others?
5. How do you respond to traditional masculinity that limits men in feeling fear and other emotions but permits them to freely express anger?

LISTENING

Steve

In conflict, we do well to follow the counsel of James: "You must understand this, my beloved: let everyone be quick to listen, slow to speak, slow to anger" (1:19 NRSVA).

In *The Seven Habits of Highly Effective People*, Stephen Covey states, "Most people do not listen to understand; they listen in order to answer. While the other is talking, they are preparing their reply."[24] Proverbs 18:13 says: "If one gives answer before hearing, it is folly and shame." Consider a story that Covey tells to illustrate folly and shame when we don't listen to understand:

> A father once told me, "I can't understand my kid. He just won't listen to me at all." "Let me restate what you just said," I replied. "You don't understand your son because *he* won't listen to *you*?" "That's right," he replied. "Let me try again," I said. "You don't understand your son because he won't listen to you?" "That's what I said," he impatiently replied. "I thought that to understand another person, *you* needed to listen to *him*," I suggested. "Oh!" he said. There was a long pause. "Oh!" he said again, as the light began to dawn. "Oh, yeah! But I do understand him. I know what he's going through. I went through the same thing myself. I guess what I don't understand is why he won't listen to me."
>
> This man didn't have the vaguest idea of what was really going on inside his boy's head. He looked into his own head and thought he saw the world, including his boy. That's the case with so many of us . . . We want to be understood. Our conversations become collective monologues, and we never really understand what's going on inside another human being.[25]

True listening seeks to understand the other. When this kind of understanding is reached, it can almost magically resolve conflicts.[26]

The Chinese symbol for listening includes five parts. Together, these parts show what is involved in deep listening:

Listen in Chinese (traditional).

- *Ears*: hearing not only words but also feelings
- *Mind*: seeking with openness and curiosity
- *Heart*: empathizing with others' feelings and needs
- *Attention*: bracketing our reactions, tending theirs
- *Eyes*: communicating "I see you"

As we're listening, we may want to recall a line from the prayer of Saint Francis: "O Divine Master, grant that I may not so much seek . . . to be understood as to understand."

> For more, see **"Spirituality of Peace"** at bit.ly/LivingThatMatters.

FOR CONVERSATION

1. When was a time someone carefully listened to you and truly understood you, and what was that like for you?
2. How quick are you to listen and how slow are you to speak? Would others close to you agree with you?
3. In your observation, how true is it that men are quick to speak and slow to listen?
4. When did understanding someone transform your perspective of them or a situation?
5. How can you improve your capacity for listening?

SPEAKING

Steve

James writes that our tongue is a small part with great power to build up or destroy—like a small fire that can set a forest ablaze. He also says the tongue is difficult to tame and master (James 3:1–12). This is especially true in conflict.

Ironically, the evening after I wrote this piece, my tongue got the best of me in a conflict with Linda, my wife. Hurt by something she said, I became angry and made a strong "you" statement, setting our bed on fire! We put the fire out, but this reminded me how hard it is to manage the tongue.

What does your tongue do in conflict? When you speak, what do you say and how do you sound to others? With listening, we seek to be attentive to others and reach understanding. With speaking, we want to help others understand us. And how we speak matters.

Of the three basic postures we can take in conflict, (1) being submissive generally does not respect our needs, can leave us feeling resentful, and often doesn't resolve conflict; (2) being aggressive generally does not respect others, may leave them feeling attacked, and may escalate the conflict; and (3) being assertive is direct and respectful and is usually the most effective. Think of it as speaking your mind while minding your speech.

With assertiveness, it's important to engage in the following tasks:

- *Separate the person from the problem.* That is, focus on the behavior, need, or issue rather than the individual or group. We may be hard on a problem, but we need to be soft on the person,[27] respecting them, remembering their identity, and inviting their cooperation.
- *Say what we mean and mean what we say.* In other words, let our yes be yes and our no be no.
- *Pay attention to the tone of our voice.* Weak and wishy-washy doesn't work well. Nor does angry and threatening. A firm, calm tone with respect is best.

Many of us have been taught to make "I" rather than "you" statements. The basic approach is to say: "I feel [*state emotion*] when [*state behavior*] because [*state effect*] I want/need [*state want or need*]."

An "I" statement expresses what I think, feel, want, or need. It does not accuse or try to control the other person. Rather than focusing on the other person, it focuses on my experience. A "you" message (often with a pointing finger) is a statement about the other person and is often blaming, which provokes a defensive reaction.

Mediator Marshall Rosenberg observes that blaming, criticizing, defending, judging, withdrawing, and attacking are common patterns in conflict. As an alternative to these patterns, he provides a four-step model for compassionate, nonviolent communication:

1. Make observations, not evaluations (judgments). Notice what I observe: "When I [*see, hear, remember, imagine*] . . ."
2. State how I feel in relation to what I observe: "I feel . . ."
3. Relate what I need or value that causes my feelings: ". . . because I need/ value . . ."
4. Make requests rather than demands. Name the specific action or actions I would like taken to meet my need: "Would you be willing to . . .?"[28]

For example, saying something like "You make me so mad. You better stop, or else . . . !" with an angry tone usually makes matters worse. A more compassionate and constructive approach speaks with a firm, calm voice: "I feel hurt when you talk to me like that. I need to be treated with respect, so when you're angry, would you please still treat me with respect?" This is more likely to produce a better response.

The point is not to memorize a formula or follow a script but to express what we think, feel, want, or need in a way that owns our experience, rather than blaming or criticizing others. We're called to "be quick to listen and slow to speak"—paying attention to our own feelings and needs before expressing ourselves. The intent is to listen and speak with one another in ways that seek mutual understanding, respect, and cooperation.

> For speaking in threatening conflicts, see **"Redirect Aggression: Assertiveness in the Way of Peace"** at bit.ly/LivingThatMatters.

🗪 FOR CONVERSATION

1. When you speak in conflict, what do you say and how do you sound to others?
2. In conflict, do you become tongue-tied, give a tongue-lashing, or do something else?
3. What makes it hard for you to stand up and speak up for yourself or others in conflict?
4. What helps you express yourself in constructive and respectful ways?

RESPONSES

Steve

How do you generally respond in conflict? And when does your response change?

As mentioned earlier, there are various styles of response to conflict. In any given conflict, those five basic styles can be mapped according to our levels of concern for (1) our goals, and (2) our relationship with those involved. Depending on these two dynamics, we will tend to accommodate, compromise, avoid, compel, or collaborate. (Individuals can take an online test to identify and learn about their primary styles of response.[29])

Here's how each of the five styles respond to conflict:[30]

Accommodate *YIELD TO THE OTHER*

Focus	Low on goal; high on relationship
How	Your way
Pro	» Open ability to negotiate now or later » Save time and effort if not important » Show you can be flexible and caring
Con	» May neglect your needs » May nurse resentment » Can perpetuate negative patterns

---

Compromise *GO PARTWAY WITH THE OTHER*

Focus	Middle on goal; middle on relationship
How	Halfway
Pro	» Show your care to the other » Invite care from the other for you » Open the way to collaboration
Con	» Partway is often not far enough » May not satisfy needs of either party

---

Avoid *WITHDRAW FROM THE OTHER*

Focus	Low on goal; low on relationship
How	No way
Pro	» Allow time to cool off or process » Withdraw from abuse or danger » Delay for right opportunity » Avoid engagement over trivial issue
Con	» May neglect the needs of both parties » May communicate lack of care » Conflict may continue or compound » Distancing or hostility may increase

Compel FORCE THE OTHER		**Collaborate** RESOLVE PROBLEM TOGETHER	
Focus	High on goal; low on relationship	**Focus**	High on goal; high on relationship
How	My way	**How**	Our way for a win-win outcome
Pro	» Secure safety for self and others » Establish basic human rights » Take quick emergency action	**Pro**	» Satisfy the needs of each party » Benefit relationship between parties » Create constructive outcomes » Provide a more sustainable solution
Con	» Control and coercion don't change hearts » Force has little influence for change » Easily escalates aggressive reactions » Easily harms relationships	**Con**	» Takes time and effort » Such processing may not be needed

Depending on the situation, relationship between parties, and goals of both parties, each of these responses has its place. Each has certain pros and cons. For example, take a family conflict over pizza toppings. Toppings are not important to me, but our family relationships are, so I will accommodate and yield to the toppings my family members want. But if on the other hand, I see someone being mistreated, I will want to compel the abusive person to stop for the safety of the person being harmed. If I'm involved with a conflict in a congregation over an important social issue, I will seek to collaborate with others, because I'm highly concerned for both the issue and our relationships. In a conflict that has become toxic and destructive, I will withdraw for necessary space. So it all depends on what style is appropriate for the situation.

For many conflicts where both the relationship and what's at stake matter, collaborating can be very effective. We address this next.

> For a map of the five main conflict styles, see **"Anatomy of Conflict and Responses"** at bit.ly/LivingThatMatters.

 FOR CONVERSATION

1. How do you generally respond in conflict? What patterns do you observe with your responses?
2. When does your response change and why?
3. What do you notice about how your conflict style works with the styles of those close to you?
4. What do you like about your style, and what would you like to change?
5. What style does our culture most reward men for? What about for other genders?

COLLABORATION

Steve

Think about transforming conflict as problem-solving. To do this well calls for collaboration—working together for a win-win outcome. Of the five styles of response to conflict, this is the one that involves important concerns and relationships. We do better when we work together. And this requires listening and speaking to discover constructive resolutions to our problems.

Imagine a stoplight directing us in relating together and resolving conflicts. The lights signal us to stop to see the problem, think how to resolve it, and act in a way to make peace with conflict.[31]

[Red] What's the problem?
• What do I think and feel?
• What does the other think and feel?

[Yellow] How can we resolve this?
• What does each of us really want?
• How can each of us get what we need?

[Green] Is this how we want to act?
• Does this meet our needs?
• Does this help our relationship?

With the red light, we want to see the problem. Here we stop and ask "What's the problem?" and consider what we think and feel as we experience the conflict or problem.

With the yellow light, we think how to resolve the problem. We answer "How can we resolve this?" by asking each other what we want, then reaching a resolution that meets both our needs.

With the green light, we consider the outcomes of our action. We ask ourselves "Is this how we want to act?" by reflecting on how our action will meet our needs and help our relationship.

In our Making Peace with Conflict retreat, we run a classic exercise with oranges: Two people have a problem when they each need the same six oranges but they don't know why the other wants the oranges. One wants to make orange juice and the other wants to make orange marmalade jam using only the peel. When told to get what they need to make what they want, participants respond in various ways and illustrate the five styles of response to conflict:

1. *Compete or compel* by grabbing all six oranges for themselves and leaving the other with nothing.
2. *Accommodate* by letting the other person have all the oranges and getting nothing for themselves.
3. *Compromise* by each taking three oranges but only getting half of what they need.
4. *Avoid* the problem all together, being conflict-avoidant, and neither gets anything while the oranges just lie there.
5. *Collaborate* by asking each other what they want with the oranges and discovering each can fully get what they need: one gets the insides for juice, and the other gets the peels for marmalade.

This is an entertaining way to witness the styles of response at play and see how collaborating helps us work together better to resolve the problem for a win-win outcome. But few figure this out until they stop and think together, discussing what they each want and need. And when they do this and discover the solution, there's often an "aha!" moment of satisfaction.

The image of the mules shows a simpler approach for working together. The moral of this model for conflict is "Cooperation is best in conflict!"

The Two Mules: A Fable for the Nation. American Friends Service Committee, 1920. Available at Library of Congress Prints and Photographs Division, #2014646806.

🗫 FOR CONVERSATION

1. The traffic light is one model for collaboration. Do you have a model that helps you?
2. When have you been stubborn in conflict, and what happened as a result?
3. What hindered you from being more collaborative?
4. Of the things you've learned about transforming conflicts, what do you want to practice?

As section 6 ends, let's stop to notice what's happening with us. After a minute of silence, discuss:

- How are we experiencing our open conversations?
- What gifts, difficulties, or tensions do we notice?
- Where is God's Spirit at work within and among us?

Life Roles

INTRODUCTION

Steve

> *What does the* LORD *require of you but to do justice*
> *and to love kindness and to walk humbly with your God?*
> **—Micah 6:8**

IN THIS FINAL SECTION, we focus on roles we play in life. Of the many roles we may serve, we address a dozen of the more common ones. These include men as sons, brothers, friends, lovers, partners, fathers, mentors, workers, leaders, stewards, activists, and elders.

While some of these are inclusive of all males, like sons and friends, others may not be for all men, like partners and fathers. In certain times and places, some roles, like leaders, have been held exclusively by males. However, as seen in various cultures, these may be served by anyone regardless of gender. In the Bible, for example, we have Huldah, Esther, and Priscilla as notable leaders.

Most of these roles have both inward and outward aspects.

As presented in the following descriptions, we usually think of the outward expression in terms of what men do and how they carry out these roles in their various settings.

The inward aspects may be thought of as that within us brought to life by something deep in our being. These parts, which some people call archetypes, are patterns, or images deep within us. From a psychological perspective, they reside in the collective unconscious inherited from generations of human experience and memory. These archetypes imprinted in our psyche energize and animate us. From a spiritual perspective, they may be seen as parts within our soul empowered by the Spirit.[1]

However understood, these parts seek to be engaged and expressed in life toward some goal. Each role has instinctual impulses, energies, and desires. For example, a warrior's are for serving and protecting. A leader's are for influencing and empowering others. A lover's are for connecting.

Each role has its gift and shadow, its bright and dark side. And each has its challenges, especially regarding how to deal with power, which can be creative or destructive.

In every age and culture, certain roles or archetypes are played out in stories, myths, and movies. Take J. R. R. Tolkien's classic *Lord of the Rings* series. Reflect on how roles are portrayed with both bright and shadow sides in this great drama. Frodo, Sam, Pippin, and Merry are loyal friends who accompany one another on their journey. Aragorn and Arwen are lovers who long for each other. Aragorn, Gimli, Legolas, and Éowyn are courageous warriors engaged in a great conflict. As king, Aragorn seeks to reestablish a peaceful order in his domain. And Gandalf is the good magician with special knowledge and powers.

Writing in the time of World War II, Tolkien witnessed the shadow side of these roles and how power can be used in violent and destructive ways. He represented this in violent warriors in the service of Sauron, their evil king, and Saruman with his foul magic.

Part of what makes a story or movie like *The Lord of the Rings* so engaging is not only its epic conflict but also the way certain parts resonate with us. While we can appreciate drama portrayed on the page of a novel or on a wide screen, we also have the opportunity to play out these roles in real life, engaging with them to bring about God's shalom.

This is what Jesus modeled. In touch with the movement of the Spirit within himself, he served most of the roles addressed in this section and played his part in serving God's shalom. Consider Jesus in the roles of friend, mentor, activist, prophet, leader, and healer among others. Carrying out his mission certainly involved conflict, confronting shadow forces, and pressing on, with a vision of God's love, justice, and peace prevailing in the end.

When we play our parts, the result likely won't be as dramatic as *Lord of the Rings* or Jesus of Nazareth. But it will be significant. When we express the movement of the Spirit through our life roles, we feel alive with a sense that our lives matter and that we make a difference.

See "Parts Men Play in Serving God's Shalom" in the resources section for a chart of our roles, biblical examples, and a list of healthy and unhealthy traits for each.

Serving in these roles is a matter of one's gifts, calling, needs, and opportunities. For discerning what roles you're to play, consider the exercises "Discerning Our Call to Service" in the resources section.

SONS

Steve

If you have the good fortune of a healthy family with loving parents, being a son is relatively easy. Consider yourself deeply blessed. Sadly, this is not the experience for many men who struggle in relating to their parents.

In men's work, father wounds are frequently cited as a source of suffering for men and a root of social problems as we act out of our pain. Richard Rohr claims that most men carry within themselves a deep father hunger or a full-blown father wound that affects them and the world.[2] Though father wounds are often predominant for sons, many men also have issues with their mothers.

These parent wounds are usually not just something in the past but often continue throughout adulthood. Focusing on our wounds can easily turn into blaming and bashing parents. This is not helpful. It just leaves us stuck in our pain and anger. If we have issues with our parents, it's better to acknowledge and address those issues in healthy ways for our healing.

In his books for wounded men, therapist John Lee openly shares his struggle of being a son and how this affects his relationships. As a wounded healer, Lee admits that healing work is difficult. He began his work first with his mother. Rather than having a mother who protected him, he had been expected to protect her from his father's abuse.

> I had supported her, when I, the child, should have been protected and provided for by her. Beginning at the tender age of five, I listened to her pain, brought her cool cloths for her migraines, and tried to counsel her. . . . My feelings of distrust for women had begun with my mother, the first and most important woman in my life. My shock of realizing this was so great that rather than process my troubling feelings, I was thrown into a deep depression.[3]

After dealing with his mother and depression, Lee turned to healing his father wound. He reports:

> It was time to work on my sadness and anger about my father. I had not seen him in several years and had never really communicated with him in my life. I denied this fact for years though I had been dreaming of my father on the average of three to five nights a week for as long as I could remember. The dreams were always filled with violence, rage, anger and hatred. The pain of the wound I received from him was too great and disturbing to remember and

bring into the light of consciousness for examination or reflection. But then I knew I must if I was going to heal myself. . . .

I began getting in touch with the rage and grief I felt toward my alcoholic, abusive father who was never around when I needed him. Even though I had convinced myself that he didn't matter to me, I hated him. I tried to do everything just the opposite of the way he had, and tried as hard as I could to never be like him. The truth was, in many ways, we were one and the same. Whenever someone pointed this out to me—usually a girlfriend or my sister—I hated it.[4]

Through counseling and other help, Lee experienced healing and found healthy ways to relate to his parents. And so can we. While reconciliation with parents is not always possible, personal healing is. To heal, learn, and move forward in life, we can

> For an exercise to deal with one's wounds, refer to **"Tending Our Wounds"** in the resources section.

- Share our experience with others
- Receive counseling for support and guidance
- Set healthy boundaries with our parents
- Work through our wounds with healing prayer
- Be the parent we wish we had (if we have children)
- Listen to the experience of our parent or parents
- Find ways to honor our parent or parents

I have struggled with parent wounds. I have found ways to deal with my anger and wounds. As a result, I feel greater freedom, peace, and love in my life. While I write this, my father is dying of cancer. Rising above issues I have had with my father, I'm seizing this opportunity to care for and honor him. I'm recording his life story, and as I listen to him, I'm learning to know and love my father in new ways, and experiencing healing between us. Closer to him now than ever, I'm learning to be a loving son and what it means to honor my parents. I wonder whether this is what Malachi had in mind when he envisioned a time when the hearts of parents are turned to their children and the hearts of children turned to their parents (Malachi 4:6).

We may be out of our parents' house, but we're sons for life. The sooner our hearts turn and heal, the sooner we may experience and extend love.

🗩 FOR CONVERSATION

1. What is (or was) your relationship with your parents like?
2. What do you appreciate about your parents?
3. What have you done or might you do to address issues you may have with your parents? (You may want to consider the "Tending Our Wounds" exercise for this.)
4. How can you love and honor your parents (whether they are alive or deceased), and what does this offer you?

BROTHERS

Steve

The Bible's first story about brothers is tragic. It speaks of spilled blood from sibling rivalry. Failing to heed God's warning to master his anger, Cain kills his brother Abel. He then flees as a fugitive, bearing the burden of his violence and slain brother. And the ground is cursed (Genesis 4:1–16).

This is not the last story of rivalry between brothers. The Bible goes on to tell about conflicts between Jacob and Esau, then Joseph and his brothers. These conflicts are drawn out over many years, with consequences rippling through generations. One of Jesus' most powerful parables features the resentment of an elder brother toward his younger "prodigal" brother.

Dramas of sibling rivalry have been played out in classic stories throughout history and across cultures, from Egyptian mythology to Shakespeare's tragedies to modern film. Brothers in conflict. Brothers competing against each other. And brothers at war. Along with these are also stories of brothers bound to their brothers and sisters in fraternal love. Reconsider the wonderful Jewish story of two brothers and the power of their brotherly love told in the "Compassion" reflection (see the Social Practices section of this book).

Powerful emotions and relational dynamics in family systems can lead to all kinds of drama. Siblings share a life history and often know each other more deeply than anyone else. So the capacity for great love and great rivalry is ever present between siblings. Given this, these relationships have the potential to be the longest loving or the longest conflicted ones in your life.

From our earliest years as brothers, we role-play what we will deal with the rest of our lives in other relationships. As brothers, we learn to deal with differences, handle hardships, recover from tragedy, transform conflict, extend forgiveness, heal brokenness, and practice love. Truly, our siblings—if we have them—influence how we perform in other relationships.

What we sometimes don't realize is that the role of brother extends beyond the circle of our biological brothers and sisters. Using the language of "family," Paul wrote that all followers of Jesus are part of one household, or family, of God. Notice how often in his letters Paul addresses believers as "brothers" and "sisters" and calls on them to care for each other as members of one another. Just as we have responsibilities as brothers in our family of origin, so is this true in our family of faith. Here also we must deal with differences, handle hardships, transform conflict, extend forgiveness, heal brokenness, and practice love with our brothers and sisters.

Jesus expanded the circle of family even further. Mark 3:31–34 tells the story of his mother and brothers coming to a house where Jesus was and calling for him. Those around Jesus say to him, "Your mother and your brothers and sisters are outside asking for you." Jesus replies by asking, "Who are my mother and my brothers?" Looking at those who sat around him, he radically redefines our larger family, saying, "Here are my mother and my brothers!" In other words, our brothers and sisters are not just those in our family of origin or even our faith community but also all those around us. This is good news for those without biological siblings or who have lost siblings from death or estrangement. We can have soul brothers and soul sisters from the world around us with whom to share our lives.

As brothers—whether in a church, another faith community, or some other group to which we belong—we have the opportunity to give and receive in our common life together. As brothers we can do our part, use our gifts, and share our resources for the good of our greater family.

Returning to the beginning of Genesis, we see the same foundational idea—that we are ultimately from one human family of God on earth. Paul holds that all people are somehow joined together in the universal Christ (Galatians 3:28). Regardless of color, culture, or creed, he proclaims, we are all one in Christ.

Imagine this: Everyone is our brother or sister! God calls us to be brothers to all—to get over our rivalry and to live in love for the well-being of the entire human family.

🗪 FOR CONVERSATION

1. If you have siblings, how would you describe your relationships with them? If you are an only child, what has that been like for you?
2. To what extent do you relate to others besides siblings as brothers or sisters (for example, in your church or faith community, volunteer group, sports, other)?
3. What have been the blessings and struggles of your relationships with your brothers and sisters (in your family of origin or another context)?
4. What difference would it make to act as loving brothers with all people in one human family?

FRIENDS

Steve

Great books and films often depict the important role of friends. Consider Sam accompanying Frodo on his journey in *The Lord of the Rings*. Frodo wouldn't have made it and completed his mission without Sam. And Frodo's recovery and joy were complete in the end only by being reunited with his friends.

The author of the Book of Sirach (in the Apocrypha) writes on the gift of being and having friends:

> Faithful friends are a sturdy shelter:
>   whoever finds one has found a treasure.
> Faithful friends are beyond price;
>   no amount can balance their worth.
> Faithful friends are life-saving medicine. (6:14–16)

The writer also describes false friendship to show what true friends are like (6:8–13). Faithful friends stand together in times of trouble. They are faithful in conflict. And they are close in adversity. When we have true friends, we can say with the writer, "Wine and music gladden the heart, but the love of friends is better than either" (40:20). The friendship between David and Jonathan illustrates this love that is intimate, steadfast, and protective (1 Samuel 18–20; 23; 2 Samuel 1).

Jesus was a true friend. Consider his concentric circles of friends and what he modeled. We think first of his twelve companions. Within this circle was the inner circle of Jesus, Peter, James, and John. And inside this circle, Jesus enjoyed his closest friendship with John, the "beloved." Even with Jesus, we see different levels of friendship. Outside the twelve, Jesus also had many other friends, like Mary, Martha, and Lazarus. Jesus looked upon them not simply as followers but also as friends. He made this clear in the end when he said, "I do not call you servants, . . . but I have called you friends" (John 15:15). When Lazarus died, Jesus cried. When others saw Jesus weeping, they exclaimed, "See how he loved him!" Here's a strong man crying over the death of a friend (John 11:35–36). Such was the love of Jesus for his friends.

Notice that Jesus chose to be with others who were significantly different from one another. For example, Jesus chose to be friends with Simon—a revolutionary Zealot—and Matthew, a tax collector and a Roman collaborator. Arguments and conflicts among the twelve disciples demonstrate that these friendships were challenging. But as we discussed earlier, conflict is simply a normal part of relationships. Rather than seeing it as a problem, Jesus saw these occasions as opportunities to learn.

Jesus formed close friendships not only with men but also with women, like Mary and Martha. This was radical for his day. With both men and women, he modeled learning and growing together as a company of companions.

In his relationships, Jesus shows us that friends embody love for one another. In being friends, we receive and extend God's love. And as we include others in our circles of belonging, we widen the embodied circle of God's love in the world.

How can we be better friends? By

- having regular habits of meeting together,
- being vulnerable in order to truly know each other,
- sharing our joys and struggles,
- extending God's unconditional love.

Being friends takes practice—that is, regular habits of being together. I have been in small groups of women and men who meet regularly to share deeply of life and faith. I have also had the weekly practice of walking with a friend at six in the morning before work. And for many years, I've met with a men's group every other week at six in the morning. Sometimes I just want to sleep in, especially on dark winter mornings, or stay home after a long day. When I look at my busy calendar or feel tired, I sometimes wonder whether it's worth the time and effort. So what keeps me going? It's what we experience together as friends by being a shelter, treasure, and medicine for one another.

> For an intentional practice of friendship, consider **"Spiritual Friendships"** in the resources section.

 FOR CONVERSATION

1. What makes someone a faithful or true friend? To what extent do you embody these traits?
2. How have friendships been a gift to you? Or, in the words of Sirach, how have friendships been a shelter, treasure, or medicine to you and others?
3. How do you practice friendship?
4. How have you been friends with others different from you, and what has this offered you?
5. What are barriers to being better friends? How much of these are related to what we're taught as men?
6. How can we strengthen and deepen our friendships in this circle and extend this to others?

LOVERS

Steve

In the beginning, God created the first humans as, among other things, lovers in the garden of Eden (Genesis 2:15–25). The image of a garden of delight is found in various ancient religions, and it features highly in Judaism, Christianity, and Islam. It is the lover's sacred space with waters and trees of life, abundant bio-diversity, and delicious fruits. Here they were, naked and unashamed, as lovers to enjoy all God had created. More than sexual partners, Adam and Eve were in intimate relationship with each other, all of creation, and God. While they enjoyed sexual love in a "one flesh" union, they delighted in all that was in the garden.

The lover is a passionate archetype and role we're meant to enjoy. While expressed in a variety of ways, the lover is about beholding, embracing, and embodying all that is sensual, beautiful, and delightful in the world. Robert Moore and Douglas Gillette write:

> The Lover is the archetype of play and of "display," of healthy embodiment, of being in the world of sensuous pleasure and in one's own body *without shame*. Thus, the Lover is *deeply sensual*—sensually aware and sensitive to the physical world in all its splendor. The Lover is related and connected to them all, drawn into them through his sensitivity. His sensitivity leads him to feel compassionately and empathetically united with them. For the man accessing the Lover, all things are bound to each other in mysterious ways.[5]

The lover feels alive with being in nature, savoring good food, connecting with others, playing with children, appreciating the arts, and enjoying sexual intimacy. As he enjoys the abundance of life, he observes the command to "eat, drink, and be merry" (Ecclesiastes 8:15 *The Living Bible*).

While God desires that we enjoy being lovers, we need to be aware of the shadow side. When a man's passion becomes an obsession, he can become possessed by the very thing he enjoys. The addicted lover is overtaken by the object of his love and its energy. What he takes, takes him. What he holds, holds him. What he possesses, possesses him. This can become destructive to him and those around him. The addicted lover is easily seen with sexual and chemical addictions when a man is driven to "get off" or get a fix. It can also happen with excessive attachment to anything that captivates our time, attention, and energy.

To prevent this, we need to enjoy things within limits and certain boundaries, following the counsel of spiritual wisdom.

In contrast with the addicted lover is the impotent lover. Rather than being possessed by passion, the impotent lover is a man out of touch with passion. He has a flattened affect in not feeling enthusiasm, excitement, or being alive. Little arouses him or makes him erect. He is left feeling flat and flaccid. What this man needs is to awaken and exercise his role as a lover! He's to recover the joy of life with what God has provided for our pleasure. He's to hear Jesus—God's Son and Lover—who said, "I came that they may have life and have it abundantly" (John 10:10).

For more on sexuality for the lover, see the Sexual Wholeness section. It's important in our men's work to deal with ourselves as addicted or impotent lovers. In Mennonite Men's Wounded Lovers retreat, we provide a space for men to address their woundedness and connect with their role as a lover so they may embrace what is good in the world as God desires.

FOR CONVERSATION

1. Where and how are you a lover in your life?
2. When was a time you felt deeply connected, at one, or in love with something or someone?
3. What do you especially enjoy that excites or arouses you with passion?
4. What object of enjoyment is or can become compulsive for you?
5. In what ways, if any, do you identify with the impotent lover?

PARTNERS

Don

In Genesis 2:18 the Creator states that being "alone" is "not good" and then sets out to create a partner for the human. This story weaves humans' natural desire for relationship into the very fabric of its telling, making it abundantly clear that we are created for relationship.[6]

While we can form relationships and live equally well with or without a life partner, here we focus on the role of partner for those who feel called to such a way of life. The forms of partnered relationships in North American society are remarkably varied and include nonsexual partnerships, unmarried sexual partnerships, same-sex marriages, and heterosexual marriages. More and more, these partnerships may include a series of "significant others" across the lifespan.

The Bible contains numerous commentaries—indirectly through stories and directly through instruction—on how partnerships function. What emerges is a view of close relationship as a place of mutual love and honoring,[7] where our often broken and shame-filled selves can be welcomed and we can experience God's beautiful intention for us—to live "naked and not ashamed" with each other (Genesis 2:25).[8] Such partnership can provide care and acceptance that are the basis of true safety.

Paul involved himself in teaching others about partnership. Taking a giant step of radical mutuality for his day, he told husbands and wives to "submit to one another" (Ephesians 5:21 NIV). Given the firm hierarchies in place at that time, this call for mutual submission between married partners—particularly for a man to submit to his wife—would have been shocking to the original recipients of his instruction. It also would have been disruptive to societal understandings of partnership.[9]

Our opportunity in healthy relationship with our significant other is to create such a place of mutual fulfillment for ourselves and our partner. This is an ongoing journey. Even after thirty-five years of partnership with my wife, I know that our relationship is and always will be a work in progress. The beauty and loving mutuality we experience together will require ongoing care and commitment for the rest of our lives in order for our partnership to continue to be meaningful.

When partners do not or cannot provide such care for their relationship, the partnership can become significantly challenging and even traumatic. Strife and pain can abound, whether through our own choices, in our families where we may have grown up as innocent bystanders, or in the community or media when private lives become public in a damaging way.

Being a good partner does not happen automatically. We must learn through others' mentoring and modeling. A client of mine recently reflected with a great deal of grief that no one had ever helped him know how to be a good husband.

Although partnerships can be places of struggle and profound pain, they can also be incredibly powerful places of healing and joy. As our understanding of human partnerships evolves over time, we are continuing to discover just what this can look like.

FOR CONVERSATION

1. What do you find meaningful about being a partner, or what would interest you about becoming a partner?
2. What do you struggle with regarding the role of partner?
3. What do you understand the Bible to be saying about partnerships? What can we learn from this for relationships today?
4. In what ways do you, or would you like to, work at mutual submission with your partner?
5. In what ways have safety and vulnerability been present and absent in your partnerships?

FATHERS

Steve

If you're a father, or a father figure for someone, what do you want for your children? As I wrote in the introduction to this book, I want our children to know who they are; to become strong, loving, and wise; and to contribute to the world.

As we seek to promote healthy masculinity, let's focus for a moment on fathering our sons. In *Boys Will Be Men*, Paul Kivel provides a vision to raise boys for a better world. He writes:

> I imagine a world in which boys are successful in school, active participants in the life of their families, and responsible members of the community. A world in which boys are strong and powerful, but also gentle and caring. . . .
>
> To create this better world, we would have to raise boys who feel connected to the environment so that they will take care of it. We would have to raise boys who are able to express a wide variety of feelings so that they can empathize with the situations of others and reach out to them with caring. . . .
> I want them to treat others with fairness and respect, and to intervene when others are being discriminated against or treated disrespectfully.[10]

It's challenging to raise boys to become such men when so much in our culture is counter to this.

When boys hear "Be a man," it often means "Be invulnerable, act tough, take control, and dominate situations." As fathers we can help rewrite these scripts and give our boys better scripts for their health and the good of others.

Kivel provides not only an important corrective to how boys are often raised but also a vision for raising all our children. Regardless of our children's gender, we want them to do well, participate in community, contribute to the world, and care for the earth. We want them to live with respect, compassion, and love. We want them to work for freedom, justice, and inclusion. We want them to stand up, speak up, and act for God's shalom. Most importantly, we want them to realize who they are as God's beloved children. We want them to know that they, along with everyone else, are created in the image of God. And we want them to be rooted and grounded in God's love.

If we want this for our children, we can help by seeking and modeling this in our own lives. We need to show what it looks like to follow the way of Jesus for God's shalom in the world. Hopefully, our children will also choose to follow Jesus for a lifestyle of love.

If we want our children to pay attention to our lives, we must be involved in theirs. Research shows that societies with involved, caring fathers are more likely than those with aloof fathers to produce positive child development and to form healthy masculinity among males, more respectful treatment of women and girls, greater gender equality, and more peaceful, less violent communities.[11] Fortunately, men are more present and involved as active caregivers from the birth experience and through the growing years than in previous generations. This has provided more opportunities for fathers to establish deeper bonds of love with their children. Being more involved may also mean experiencing more pain and difficulty.[12] Despite the challenges, we will likely experience greater love if we are involved with our children than if we are distant from them.

A few final tips on parenting. Say "I love you." Give lots of affection and affirmation. Nurture your children's esteem by reinforcing that a person's worth comes from who they are and not their appearance, performance, or ability. Show respect to their mother and your partner or spouse. Remember that what is *caught* (from example) is more influential than what is *taught* (from instruction). When (not if) you mess up, fess up. Admit your mistakes, apologize, and make amends. Know there's no such thing as a perfect father, so seek to be a good father. Keep doing your work to grow in strength, love, and wisdom—which will encourage your children. And find ways to bless your children throughout life.[13]

If you are a father, you have an important role of helping your children become who God created them to be, enjoy a good life, and build a better world.

⯅⯅ FOR CONVERSATION

1. What do you want for your (biological, adopted, or otherwise) children?
2. What are you doing with and for them to nurture their development? And what are you modeling?
3. Do you tend to focus more on providing for your children or being with your children?
4. What are your joys and struggles as a father or father figure?

MENTORS

Steve

According to the *Oxford English Dictionary*, the term *mentor* involves the following meanings: "Originally, a person who acts as guide and adviser to another person, esp. one who is younger and less experienced. Later, more generally: a person who offers support and guidance to another; an experienced and trusted counsellor or friend; a patron, a sponsor."

Think of someone who was a mentor to you—a guide who encouraged you and showed you the way. Recall how important he or she was in supporting or equipping you so you could progress in life. Now consider how you can do this for others.

Being a mentor is an important role that we serve to support, guide, or train others in their faith, life, and work. Mentoring may be expressed through formal roles we have in our workplace, community, or congregation. It also often happens through informal relationships.

The apostle Paul was an important mentor to young Timothy, as we find in the letters of 1 and 2 Timothy. What can we learn from Paul's example about mentoring others in their faith and life? For those we mentor, embrace the following actions:

- *Regard them with loving respect.* Paul had not only respect but also affection for Timothy as a "beloved child" (2 Timothy 1:2). He reminded Timothy of who he was as God's beloved child. Such respect and affection expressed to younger people, along with reminders of their identity, encourages them in their development.
- *Affirm what God is forming in their lives.* Paul commended Timothy's faith and encouraged him to develop gifts God had given him. He pointed to God's Spirit, who makes us strong, loving, and wise (2 Timothy 1:5–7).
- *Share your experiences of faith and life.* Paul openly shared about God, his own call, and his life struggles. As he did this, he offered a model of growing as a follower of Jesus (2 Timothy 1:8–14).
- *Encourage training in Christian character.* Paul said bodily training has some benefit, and then pointed to the greater value of spiritual training to grow in love and faith (1 Timothy 4:7–16).
- *Guide them away from pitfalls and toward the good life.* Paul warned of

deadly traps such as the love of money that result in ruin, and he commended pursuing the good life God wants us to enjoy (1 Timothy 6:6–12).

Henri Nouwen was an important mentor for his nephew Marc. When Marc was nineteen and struggling with issues of faith and spirituality, Nouwen corresponded with him through letters. In one letter, Nouwen wrote, "If I were to let my life be taken over by what is urgent, I might never get around to what is essential. It's so easy to spend your whole time being preoccupied with urgent matters and never starting to live, really to live, at all." He also stated, "I want to give you a taste of the richness of life as a Christian as I know it, undergo it and continue to discover it. I really do believe that I have something of importance to tell you, and I'm very pleased to be able to do so. It's grand to be able to put across what to me is most precious to someone who is happy to hear it."[14]

Like Paul and Nouwen, we have something to share with young people, and they have something to share with us. Mentoring provides a mutual benefit when we allow young people to touch our lives as we touch theirs. This is what mentoring can be: deeply sharing what matters in life.

FOR CONVERSATION

1. Who were or are influential mentors in your life?
2. What did they do with and for you that was important?
3. How are you mentoring others?
4. How can we be more intentional in mentoring others?

WORKERS

Don

For many men, no role may dominate their waking hours more than that of worker. The usual response to "Tell me a little about you" will often be some description of our work life: "I'm a farmer"; "I'm an engineer"; "I'm a construction worker"; "I'm a teacher"; "I'm a pastor."

So much of male identity has been wrapped up in employment, productivity, and earning a living for oneself and one's family. A sense of worth or self-esteem teeters on having a job, and better yet, the right job. Leaving or losing a job can trigger a significant identity crisis. For some men, work brings much reward and accomplishment, with the greatest meaning when it serves a sense of vocation—that is, when our work is aligned with our calling to serve something bigger. For others, work life brings years of drudgery, risk, and sometimes even death.

For boys and young men, coming of age has generally demanded pursuing some form of employment or career. Disruption of this path, especially in times of social and economic uncertainty, leaves many young men confused and distraught. I regularly encounter young men in my practice who are completely disillusioned and deeply depressed because they haven't met the social expectations of becoming independent and self-sufficient through conventional education or employment.

At the other end of life are those whose employment has been interrupted by economics or life circumstances that leave them unmoored and lacking purpose. For some men, the prospect of retirement might mean a crisis of financial uncertainty or meaninglessness as they face the loss of not only a regular paycheck but also their identity tied to a trade, or company, or colleagues who have been their only friends in life.

A life of work creates many demands on a man's selfhood. Choosing a job that will bring in enough money to support self and family may require letting go of one's interests and passions. This can result in a lifelong trap of working an unfulfilling job to meet financial responsibilities.[15] Employment opportunities may bring us in direct conflict with our values: the boss directing an accountant to "fudge" the books; or a demand to dump toxic substances down the sewer. Work may also require leaving family for extended periods.

If you are a boss, an owner, or an entrepreneur, financial risks accompany the possibilities of riches; long hours and stress are often required for success; and in many ways, even more direct ethical dilemmas become yours.

Work/life balance is critical. Too often, however, circumstances leave few choices, and such balance becomes an out-of-reach privilege. Economics that demand long hours and multiple jobs—often in precarious employment situations—stretch capacities and take a toll on physical and emotional health. This leaves limited time for family and personal pursuits and can turn into workaholism. Workaholism is a specific form of compulsive behavior that is particularly problematic because society often rewards working hard and for long hours.

For those who reach retirement from formal work life with health and adequate financial resources, getting involved in meaningful activities can be deeply satisfying. Engaging in opportunities such as volunteer work, part-time employment, hobbies, or service work can enrich people as they spend their time according to interest and passion rather than being tied to just making a living.

For Christian men, work has often been elevated as a sign of godliness, and the lack of work has been viewed as a source of shame. The messages about responsibility and productivity have been plentiful, inspired by several biblical texts (see Colossians 3:23; Proverbs 14:23; 16:3; Genesis 2:15; Ecclesiastes 9:10). Ultimately, however, we must recognize that our worth depends not on our work but on who we are with God. Thankfully, we are developing a healthier understanding of the importance of balancing our lives; the toll of meaningless or excessive work; and the breadth of meaning in our lives as men that opens us to a fuller self-identity.

We are workers, yes, and we are also so much more!

👥 FOR CONVERSATION

1. What role has work played in your life?
2. To what extent does your worth depend on your work?
3. In what ways, if at all, has your work brought you into conflict with values of family, ethical choices, work/life balance, workaholism?
4. How have you managed to develop meaning within and beyond your life as a worker?

LEADERS

Steve

Leaders are persons who, in their relationships and groups, influence the thoughts, attitudes, and behaviors of others. Broadly defined, leadership is any attempt to influence other individuals or groups.[16]

No matter our gender, we may be leaders in our homes, professions, congregations, communities, and organizations. In these places, we seek to accomplish the well-being and growth of our group while working for the common good. As followers, we're called to cooperate with leaders in our lives so that together we may be successful in our endeavors.

Men have accomplished much good in the world as leaders. We recognize and appreciate this. Men have also often abused leadership roles to violate and oppress women, people of color, and marginalized groups. We must acknowledge this and carefully consider how we lead and what our impact is on others.

As we lead, we exercise power to influence others and make things happen. But leaders, especially those in positions with authority, are not often aware of their power and how they exercise it.[17] When we lead, it's critical for us to be aware of our power and its effects. It matters how we use our power, because what we do with it can be creative or destructive.

Consider the following kinds of power we might use:

- Power *with*—joining others to achieve some good
- Power *for*—serving needs and interests of others
- Power *over*—dominating or controlling others
- Power *against*—violating the well-being of others

We're to use power *with* and *for*, not *over* and *against* others. Leaders too often abuse their power for personal gain, to control others, and to oppress groups. This is especially true for men taught to take charge and dominate others. These men tend to use power over and against rather than with and for others.

The New Testament illustrates these differences with Herod and Jesus. Herod ruled as an oppressive king, using fear and power over and against others to control his subjects. In contrast, Jesus led as a good shepherd, using love and his powers to serve others. Even though he was God's anointed messiah and king, Jesus made it clear that leaders are to use their position and power to serve and not lord over others (Matthew 20:20–28; Luke 22:25–27; John 13:1–15; cf. Philippians 2:5–8).

Based on the example of Jesus, Robert Greenleaf, former CEO of AT&T, called for and modeled servant leadership. He defined leadership as a philosophy and set of practices that enrich the lives of people, build better organizations, and ultimately create a more just and caring world. He set forth these test questions for leaders:

- Do those served grow as persons? Do they, while being served, become healthier, wiser, freer, more autonomous, more likely themselves to become servants?
- And, what is the effect on the least privileged in society? Will they benefit or at least not be further deprived?[18]

We need to ask these questions of ourselves wherever we lead. And we need to ask these of leaders who govern our cities, states, and nations. Leaders today join kings and queens throughout history in playing an important part in creating a just and caring world. They are to protect human rights, serve human needs, and advance social development in their domain.[19]

In Psalm 72, a royal psalm for a king's coronation, we see the role of political leaders. They are to rule with justice, defend the poor, deliver the needy, stop the oppressor, and save people from violence so that justice may flourish and peace abound. The Old Testament holds up King David and Queen Esther as models of leaders who used their office and power to rule well.

When it comes to election time, we need servant leaders who put others first rather themselves as they pursue a social order of peace with justice. Think of great leaders like W. L. Mackenzie King in Canada, Abraham Lincoln in the United States, Corazon Aquino in the Philippines, Angela Merkel in Germany, Ellen Johnson Sirleaf in Liberia, and Julius Nyerere in Tanzania. We need more leaders like these to govern our world well.

And in our settings we need to be servant leaders to create God's shalom. To this end, as we lead, let us be strong, loving, and wise.

For more on power, see **Power** in the Conflict Tools section of this book.

FOR CONVERSATION

1. Where and in what ways do you lead?
2. Do you like being a leader or do you shy away from leadership? Why?
3. How do you tend to exercise power—with and for, or over and against others?
4. What does being strong, loving, and wise look like in leadership? Who exemplifies these traits for you?

STEWARDS

Steve

Psalm 24:1 proclaims this important truth: "God owns this planet and all its riches. The earth and every creature belongs to God."[20]

Judging from our lifestyles, one might think we own the planet. But we don't. God does. We are stewards of what belongs to God. When we think about our role as God's stewards, we often focus on rightly managing our time, gifts, and money. We recognize everything comes from God and has been entrusted to us to use well. We hope to hear what the servant heard in Jesus' parable of the talents: "Well done, good and faithful servant . . . come and share your master's joy" (Matthew 25:23 NCB).

God has graciously given us much and invites us to freely share what we have for the well-being of the world. Based on the way Jesus gave of himself, New Testament practice of generous giving (2 Corinthians 8:1–9:15) replaced the Old Testament expectation of calculated tithing. Following this, we seek to practice generosity in sharing what we have with others.

As important as it is to be generous stewards of our money, time, and talent, the role of steward first had to do with tending the earth. God's very first command to humankind was to be fruitful and multiply, and to have dominion over God's creatures (Genesis 1:28).[21] Unfortunately, dominion has been taken to mean domination and exploitation of the earth. One translation expresses the true meaning of this verse: "Let them be stewards . . . and be responsible . . ." (*The Inclusive Bible*). Being responsible stewards of God's creation is more important than ever. As a direct consequence of our earth-damaging lifestyles, climate change—more than anything else—threatens human life and biodiversity on the planet.

Aldo Leopold observed long ago that "we abuse land because we regard it as a commodity belonging to us. When we see land as a community to which we belong, we may begin to use it with love and respect."[22] Rather than thinking we own the planet and can do with its resources as we please, we need to assume our role as faithful stewards of God's earth. We read in Genesis 2:15 that God put the human in the garden of Eden to serve and protect it so that it would be fruitful.[23] As stewards, we're to tend God's creation. We have the responsibility, privilege, and joy of caring for the earth in ways that nurture and preserve the beauty, biodiversity, and abundance God intends.

Robin Wall Kimmerer, in her compelling book *Braiding Sweetgrass: Indigenous Wisdom, Scientific Knowledge, and the Teaching of Plants*, presents a Native American approach to living on the earth. Consider Indigenous stewardship with its similarities to biblical practice. In contrast to modern capitalism that exploits the earth and uses its resources as commodities, Indigenous cultures care for the earth and treat its goods as the Creator's gifts to be shared for the whole community. The Indigenous "One Bowl and One Spoon" teaching "holds that the gifts of the earth are all in one bowl, all to be shared from a single spoon. This is the vision of the economy of the commons, wherein resources fundamental to our well-being, like water and land and forests, are commonly held rather than commodified."[24]

As life on earth is increasingly threatened by economic disparities and climate changes, we would do well to recognize that all things are interconnected in the community of creation. We all share from one bowl on one earth with its resources. Remembering this, we aim to be good stewards of what God has entrusted to our care.

> See **"Caring for the Earth"** at bit.ly/LivingThatMatters.
> To help restore the earth with our campaign to plant one million trees, see JoinTrees at MennoniteMen.org.
> On financial stewardship, see **"Stewardship of Our Financial Resources"** at bit.ly/LivingThatMatters.

 FOR CONVERSATION

1. Do you tend to be a stingy or a generous steward of your money, time, and talent? Why?
2. How do you care for God's endangered earth?
3. What invitations do you hear for being a steward?

ACTIVISTS

Steve

Before "activists," there were warriors with a role to serve and protect. *Activist* is a new word from the past century for those who use strong actions for social or environmental causes. Based on the Latin root for doing or driving force, the term is used for those engaged in forceful actions for important aims.

In *Wildmen, Warriors, and Kings*, Patrick Arnold notes that "traditional society and religion once honored and ordered male aggressiveness by creating an entire mythos, ritual, and ethical code system around its principle spiritual archetype, the Warrior. Once it was a high honor for a man to say, 'I am a Warrior.'"[25]

Of all the archetypes and roles of men, the warrior is the most difficult for Anabaptist men in the peace church tradition.[26] What place, if any, does the warrior have for us who follow the nonviolent way of Jesus? I think it's an important role in the service of God's shalom.

In the Peacemakers martial arts academy I directed, we drew on warrior traditions in martial arts training for empowering students to prevent violence and transform conflict.[27] We taught the way of Sensei Ueshiba, the founder of aikido, who taught that the art of peace relies not on brute force but on the power of love. He held that the defining traits of a true warrior are true courage, love, and wisdom.[28]

By definition, warriors are not just those involved in warfare but also those engaged in conflict or struggle. For example, Martin Luther King Jr. was widely upheld as a nonviolent warrior for social justice engaged in the civil rights struggle.

Yahweh was seen as a warrior (Exodus 15:3; Zephaniah 3:17) to protect people, fight injustice, liberate from oppression, and bring about justice. Old Testament warriors include Moses, Miriam, Joshua, Deborah, Jael, Gideon, and David. The source of warrior power is not in their strength but in God's presence (Judges 6:7–17; Psalm 33:16) and wisdom (Proverbs 24:5). Warriors were nonviolent in the beginning and end of the Bible; it's in the middle of the narrative that warriors committed violence in fighting for God—which is seen as a failure to trust God.[29] Jesus claimed the Messiah's mission (Luke 4:18–19), confronted evil, cleared the temple, and spoke truth to powers.[30] In Revelation, the Christ is the divine warrior wielding not a blade of steel but the sword of God's word to defeat evil and establish God's reign.[31]

Created in God's image, followers of Jesus may identify with this warrior role, impulse, and energy to serve and protect. While I think there's a place for nonviolent, peaceful warriors, I understand that the use of "warriors" or this archetype, with its violent and militant connotations, is problematic for some people. So let's go with "activists" for our role to engage in forceful, nonviolent action for important causes. This challenges us to move beyond passive nonresistance to active, nonviolent action in advancing God's shalom.[32]

Peaceful activists don't wait for things to happen; they catalyze change with action. Think of activists like Mahatma Gandhi, Martin Luther King Jr., Rosa Parks, Oscar Romero, Corazon Aquino, and Benazir Bhutto.[33] Forceful activists like these demonstrate the transforming power of nonviolent action.

Peaceful activists are devoted to a greater good, "fight" for what is right, defend people and the planet. In various missions to advocate and protect, they are seen in human and environmental rights groups like Black Lives Matter, Greenpeace, the Water Protectors of Standing Rock, and Christian (now Community) Peacemaker Teams.[34] By contrast, violent activists or warriors act with intimidation, aggression, and domination. They promote violence, and are seen in gangs, militant groups, and events like the insurrection in Washington, DC, on January 6, 2021.

It's easy for activists to get caught up in conflicts and violent reactions. This is why it's important to engage in action with a code of conduct. For example, our Engaging the Warrior retreat closes with this pledge:

As a nonviolent warrior, I will
respect the sacredness of all life,
act with discipline and courage,
stand up, speak up, and do my part,
protect all people and our planet,
establish God's peace with justice,
serve with devotion and honor,
all in the name of Christ and
in the strength of God's Spirit.

> For additional resources, see **"Nonviolence"** in the Conflict Tools section of this book and **"The Biblical Call to Nonviolence and Peace"** at bit.ly/LivingThatMatters.

Whatever we seek to advance or protect, our call is to be peaceful activists who follow the way of Jesus in the power of the Spirit for God's shalom.

FOR CONVERSATION

1. Where have you seen activists bring about something good?
2. What about activists resonates within you?
3. How have you engaged as an activist in your life?
4. Who or what might you be called to serve and protect?

ELDERS

Steve

One of the last important roles we play in life is that of an elder. Mature men in the second half of life have the opportunity to model what it looks like to be strong, loving, and wise and offer the gifts of our life experience. Being an elder is not only for a few in certain positions but for all mature adults, of any gender, in the community.

In the final stages of life, we are destined to be not just elderly but also elders. While our bodies may decline, we can still embody virtues and share of our lives. We can take heart by focusing not on negative aspects of aging but on the generative opportunities of "sage-ing." In the end, we can finish life as holy or whole human beings others can look to as sages who know abundant life.

While Western society that is preoccupied with work, productivity, and achievement may not value elders, most traditional cultures hold this role in high esteem.

In *The Elder Within: The Source of Mature Masculinity*, Terry Jones writes, "The move away from the *doingness* of our earlier years into the *beingness* of the second half of life does not mean that elders are passive."[35] Our later years can be an adventure in eldership. This is not a time of depletion but of generativity as we are stewards of life for others and the planet.

What do elders offer others and themselves? They

- know who they are as God's beloved sons;
- nurture their formation with spiritual practices;
- accept their limitations with humility and grace;
- express the power of love over the love of power;
- mentor rather than direct others;
- affirm, encourage, and bless others;
- offer a generative, life-giving presence.

When David retired from his active years as a leader, he became a wise elder, as seen in his wisdom psalms.

Jesus was a young elder, wise from experience in living with God. Seeing Jesus as a great rabbi or sage, people wanted his wisdom, and they wanted to be whole. They wanted to know how to live life.

John was one of only a few disciples who grew to an old age. His gospel and letters reflect his wisdom as elder. For example, he came to deeply know the following life-giving truth and conveyed it to his community:

> See what love Abba God has lavished on us in letting us be called God's children! Yet that in fact is what we are. . . . My dear friends, now we are God's children, but it has not been revealed what we are to become in the future. We know that when it comes to light, we will be like God, for we will see God as God really is. (1 John 3:1–2 *The Inclusive Bible*)

The enlightened elder wants us to know and become who we are. This is distilled wisdom from one who knows life in God.

Rabbi Zalman Schachter-Shalomi writes of elders:

> They are wisdom keepers who have an ongoing responsibility for maintaining society's well-being and safeguarding the health of our ailing planet Earth. They are pioneers in consciousness who practice contemplative arts from our spiritual traditions to open up greater intelligence for their late-life vocations. Using tools for inner growth, such as meditation, journal writing, and life review, elders come to terms with their mortality, harvest the wisdom of their years, and transmit a legacy to future generations. Serving as mentors, they pass on the distilled essence of their life experience to others. The joy of passing on wisdom to younger people not only seeds the future, but crowns an elder's life with worth and nobility.[36]

If we aspire to finish life well as mature men, seek to become wise elders. To this end, follow in the way of Jesus. Seek God's shalom for all people and the planet. Enjoy and extend God's abundant life of freedom, love, and peace. Share the gifts we have received. Be a generative presence in our communities. And bless others. In the end, may we finally rest in God's Spirit, who makes us strong, loving, and wise.

FOR CONVERSATION

1. Who are elders that you hold in high esteem, and why?
2. What are you doing to develop the elder within you?
3. How and with whom are you being an elder?
4. What wisdom or gifts do you offer others?
5. How does it help to reframe aging as sage-ing?

As section 7 ends, let's stop to notice what's happening with us. After a minute of silence, discuss:

- How are we experiencing our open conversations?
- What gifts, difficulties, or tensions do we notice?
- Where is God's Spirit at work within and among us?

Resources

Discerning Our Call to Service

Discerning My Personal Mission

How I Experience Conflict

Parts Men Play in Serving God's Shalom

Reconstructing Masculinities

Sexual Integrity

Spiritual Friendships

Tending Our Wounds

For more resources, go to
bit.ly/LivingThatMatters

DISCERNING OUR CALL TO SERVICE

*The place God calls you is where your deep gladness
and the world's hunger meet.*
—**Frederick Buechner,** *Wishful Thinking: A Seeker's ABC*

Deep gladness

1. Awareness of self
   a. What did you love to do as a child? (Ask your parents, if possible.)
   b. What are you good at? What special abilities or resources have you been given?
   c. What intrigues you? What do you want to read about and learn about?
   d. At the end of the day, where do you have the sense that "I was the right person in the right place at the right time"?
   e. Where has God touched and healed a broken place in your life so that you might also understand and touch others?
2. Awareness of others
   a. What gifts and talents do others see in you that you might not see?
   b. For what do others thank or recognize you?
   c. In what situations do others turn to you for help or inspiration?
   d. What do people see as your ministry?
3. Awareness of God
   a. When do you sense God smiling and saying, "You are my beloved child with whom I am well pleased"?
   b. What part of Jesus' life and ministry most attracts and intrigues you?
   c. What do you sense God asking you to be or to do?
   d. In what ways are you involved in the work of the church?
   e. In what ways are you involved in the larger community?

The world's hunger

1. The world hungers for the light of Love in all places:
   In your home and in your friendships
   In your work and in your volunteering
   In your local and global community
   a. How can you embody Jesus' presence in the world?
   b. What hurts need to be cared for?
   c. What outsider needs to be included?
   d. What misunderstanding needs to be seen in God's way?
   e. What injustice needs your advocacy and intervention?
   f. Who in your life needs Jesus' ministries—of preaching, teaching, prayer, care, welcome, forgiveness, healing, and hope?
2. The world is hungry for the church to truly be the body of Christ.
   a. What part of the life of the church do you connect with most?
   b. What gifts do you have that the church needs or can use?

God's call merges deep gladness with the world's hunger

We believe in God's ability to work through us.
1. Where in your life can you most vividly imagine God working through you and your gifts to accomplish God's will on earth?
2. We cannot do all things. Of all the things you might do, where do you sense God nudging you right now?

Adapted by Steve Thomas and Walnut Hill Mennonite Church (Goshen, IN) from Nina Lanctot, "Discerning God's Gifts and Our Calling."

DISCERNING MY PERSONAL MISSION

Steve

Our overall purpose in life is to *enjoy and extend God's abundant life of freedom, love, and peace.* How we express this varies from person to person in the roles we serve. We discover our personal mission when we align our aspirations with God's purpose to establish shalom in the world. This involves prayerfully listening to our hearts for what gives us life, seeing how our gifts intersect with some need, and hearing feedback from others to clarify our call.

Step 1: What do I love to do?

To know your aspirations, ask yourself:
As a child, what absorbed me in play?
When do I feel energized and most alive?
What do I secretly dream of doing?
If I had only one year to live, what would I do?

What common things emerge with your answers to these questions?

Aspiration action words

Identify action words that reflect your aspirations. Underline words in the columns that fit you. Then, from these underlined words, circle one to three verbs or actions that best express what gives your life meaning and joy.

• Accomplish	• Conceive	• Enliven	• Laugh	• Promote
• Acquire	• Connect	• Entertain	• Launch	• Provide
• Act	• Construct	• Enthuse	• Lead	• Pursue
• Adopt	• Counsel	• Evaluate	• Learn	• Read
• Advance	• Create	• Excite	• Live	• Realize
• Advocate	• Debate	• Explore	• Love	• Receive
• Affirm	• Decide	• Express	• Make	• Reclaim
• Alleviate	• Defend	• Extend	• Manifest	• Reconcile
• Analyze	• Delight	• Facilitate	• Master	• Reduce
• Appreciate	• Deliver	• Finance	• Mediate	• Refine
• Bake	• Demonstrate	• Foster	• Model	• Reflect
• Believe	• Design	• Gather	• Mold	• Reform
• Bestow	• Develop	• Generate	• Motivate	• Relate
• Brighten	• Devise	• Give	• Move	• Relax
• Build	• Direct	• Grant	• Negotiate	• Release
• Call	• Discover	• Guide	• Nurture	• Remember
• Cause	• Distribute	• Heal	• Open	• Renew
• Choose	• Draft	• Hold	• Organize	• Resonate
• Claim	• Dream	• Host	• Participate	• Respect
• Coach	• Drive	• Identify	• Perform	• Restore
• Collaborate	• Educate	• Illuminate	• Persuade	• Return
• Collect	• Embrace	• Implement	• Play	• Revise
• Combine	• Encourage	• Improve	• Possess	• Sacrifice
• Command	• Endow	• Improvise	• Practice	• Safeguard
• Communicate	• Engage	• Inspire	• Praise	• Satisfy
• Compete	• Engineer	• Integrate	• Prepare	• Save
• Complete	• Enhance	• Involve	• Present	• Sell
• Compliment	• Enjoy	• Keep	• Produce	• Serve
• Compose	• Enlighten	• Know	• Progress	

Write the word or words you circled.

I love to . . .

Step 2: What do I deeply value?

Values are those things we regard as having ultimate worth, importance, or significance in life. These values may include the following:

• Beauty	• Honor	• Justice	• Service
• Compassion	• Hope	• Knowledge	• Simplicity
• Diversity	• Hospitality	• Leisure	• Sustainability
• Equality	• Humor	• Love	• Truth
• Faith	• Inclusion	• Order	• Wisdom
• Freedom	• Integrity	• Peace	• Other:
• Generosity	• Joy	• Resourcefulness	

To know your core values, ask yourself:

What are my action words (above in step 1) directed at?

What principles, causes, or qualities am I devoted to?

What's most important to me?

I deeply value . . .

Step 3: Who or what am I here to serve?

To see who and what you're here to serve, ask yourself:
Who needs what I have to offer?
Who or what do I care most about?
Who or what am I drawn to?

I am here to serve . . .

Step 4: Write your mission statement.

Write one sentence that puts your responses above together. For now, this is your personal mission statement in life.

My mission is to . . .

For more, see Dennis Linn, Sheila Fabricant Linn, and Matthew Linn, Healing the Purpose of Your Life *(Paulist, 1999); Laurie Beth Jones,* The Path: Creating Your Mission Statement for Work and for Life *(Hyperion, 1998); and Richard Nelson Bolles,* What Color Is Your Parachute? *(Ten Speed Press, 2015).*

HOW I EXPERIENCE CONFLICT

Steve

For me, conflict is like . . .

- ☐ **War** . . . where I'm engaged in a life-and-death battle against an enemy
- ☐ **Competition** . . . where I'm competing against an opponent
- ☐ **A bomb** . . . where I'm facing the danger of a violent explosion
- ☐ **Juggling** . . . where I'm trying to carefully balance a number of objects
- ☐ **A trial** . . . where I'm being tried to determine innocence or guilt
- ☐ **A dance** . . . where I'm learning to move in step with my partner or others
- ☐ **A game** . . . where I'm playing by friendly rules and want to win
- ☐ **Negotiation** . . . where I'm at a bargaining table negotiating an agreement
- ☐ **A puzzle** . . . where I'm sorting and putting pieces together to complete a picture
- ☐ **A problem** . . . where I'm challenged to discover a resolution to a difficulty
- ☐ **A dilemma** . . . where I'm caught between two unfavorable "horns" or options
- ☐ **An adventure** . . . where I'm on an exciting venture of exploration and discovery
- ☐ **A maze** . . . where I'm trying to find my way through or out
- ☐ **A storm** . . . where I'm seeking cover from destructive forces
- ☐ **A tide** . . . where I'm facing powerful but predictable forces that are natural
- ☐ **Firefighting** . . . where I'm trying to contain a fire from spreading
- ☐ **A volcano** . . . where I'm wondering whether hot gases and lava are about to erupt
- ☐ **A garden** . . . where I'm tending wanted seeds and plants but also weeds and pests
- ☐ **Other:** _____

Optional: **Draw an image that represents conflict for you. What does this image express?**

For me, conflict is like . . .

In conflict, I often feel . . .

☐ Angry   ☐ Lonely   ☐ Ashamed
☐ Aggressive   ☐ Sick   ☐ Energized
☐ Sad   ☐ Indifferent   ☐ Resentful
☐ Optimistic   ☐ Superior   ☐ Hopeful
☐ Excited   ☐ Isolated   ☐ Hostile
☐ Inferior   ☐ Cautious   ☐ Stressed
☐ Intimidated   ☐ Hurt   ☐ Enthusiastic
☐ Fearful   ☐ Guilty   ☐ Other: _____

As for my assumptions, I believe conflict is . . .

☐ inevitable and experienced by all
☐ abnormal, and harmony is normal
☐ a natural part of God's creation
☐ a result of our sin
☐ a problem to be avoided
☐ an opportunity to be explored

For further consideration: **Ask yourself these questions and see where it takes you.**

In conflict, my family often . . .

In conflict, I often . . .

PARTS MEN PLAY
IN SERVING GOD'S SHALOM

Steve

Parts are common roles in scripture and archetypes (psychic patterns with instinctual energies) for human formation and service. Jesus, the image of God and model human, fulfilled these parts as he served his mission of extending God's shalom.

Part	Role	Symbol	Examples	Healthy traits	Unhealthy traits
Steward	Tend the earth as a keeper of God's creation	Shovel	Adam	Attentive, responsible, and nurturing in caring for the land	Exploitive of the earth and its resources, destructive
Warrior	Serve and pro-tect all people and our world	Sword	Moses, Joshua, Gideon, David	Disciplined, engaged, sacrificial, loyal, courageous, and assertive	Sadistic, aggressive, dominating, destructive, violent
Lover	Delight in what is lovely and beautiful	Heart, phallus	David, Jonathan, Solomon	Sensual, loving, passionate, connected, appreciative, faithful	Addicted, narcissistic, possessive, promiscuous, controlling
Partner	Live with a companion in a committed relationship	Coven-ant	Joseph	Loving, loyal, caring, inti-mate, support-ive, committed	Selfish, jealous, possessive, controlling
Father	Nurture, guide, love, and bless one's family	Hand	Abraham, Jacob	Encouraging, affectionate, nurturing, sup-portive, loving	Controlling, dominating

Part	Role	Symbol	Examples	Healthy traits	Unhealthy traits
Mentor	Guide others along their journey as they mature	Hand	Elijah, Elisha, Paul, Barnabas	Encouraging, supportive, affirming, loving	Controlling, dominating
Healer	Restore health and wholeness in acts of care	Vial	Elisha	Discerning, knowledgeable, understanding	Exploitive, coercive
Prophet	Address issues with God's word and will	Pen	Jeremiah, Isaiah, Amos, Micah, John the Baptist	Discerning, passionate, assertive, understanding, insightful	Depressive, pessimistic, despairing
Leader	Influence and empower others	Staff	Moses, David, Solomon	Empowering, just, generative, secure, authoritative	Tyrannical, insecure, controlling, exploitive
Elder	Embody and extend wisdom	Gray hair	Abraham, Elijah, Paul, John	Trusting, centered, generative, gracious, wise	Old fool or bitter man with little learning or growth

RECONSTRUCTING MASCULINITIES

Steve

Recognizing that "men" and "masculinity" are socially constructed, let's consider the making of men.

A. Traditional masculinity: The Man Box of so-called real men

Thinking of our dominant culture of traditional masculinity, write the marks of a "real man" inside the box. Outside the box, write what males are called who don't fit in the Man Box.

A Real Man . . .

DISCUSSION QUESTIONS

1. Which of these traits can be healthy? Which of these may be a problem?
2. How are boys and men boxed in or controlled by these social definitions?
3. How are boys and men treated when they don't fit these social norms? How does this affect them?
4. How does this kind of masculinity look at and relate to people of other genders? How does this affect them?

B. Healthy masculinities: The circle of good men

Imagining healthy masculinity, write characteristics of a good man within the circle. Consider what Jesus embodied and how he related to others.

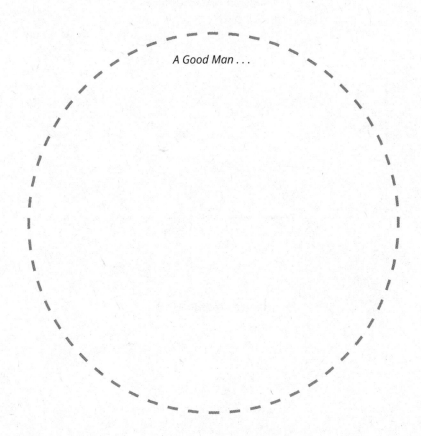

A Good Man . . .

DISCUSSION QUESTIONS

1. Which of these traits are especially important for Anabaptists?
2. What difference might it make in how we're formed as males to define healthy masculinity in these terms?
3. What difference might it make in the world for males and people of other genders if men lived out this kind of masculinity?
4. What kind of man do you want to be? What would you want said at your memorial service or funeral, reflecting on your life as a good man?

If desired, pull together findings from this exercise to create summary lists of traditional masculinity and healthy masculinity.

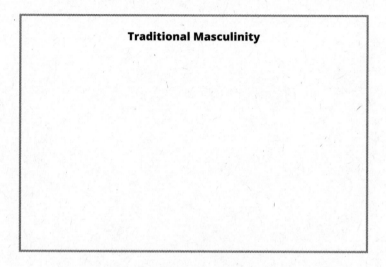

Traditional Masculinity

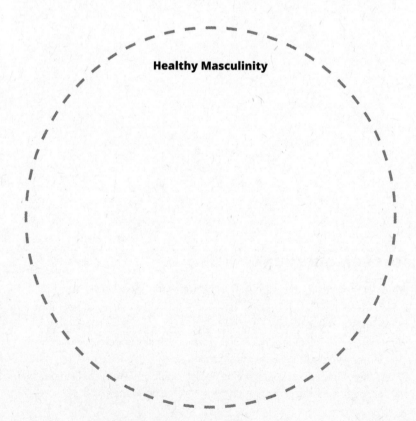

Healthy Masculinity

You might compare this to what bell hooks, drawing on the work of Olga Silverstein and Ronald Levant, describes in *The Will to Change: Men, Masculinity, and Love* (Washington Square Press, 2004), 118.

Traditional masculinity is about . . .

avoiding femininity

restrictive emotionality

seeking achievement and status

self-reliance

aggression

homophobia

nonrelational approaches to sexuality

This kind of masculinity denies men their full humanity and destroys their own and others' well-being.

Healthy masculinity is about . . .

integrity

self-love

emotional awareness

assertiveness

empathy and strength

autonomy and connectedness

responsibility to self, family, and society

This kind of masculinity creates and sustains life and peace.

SEXUAL INTEGRITY

As human beings, we are both animals driven by sexual instincts and persons longing for sexual intimacy. We are men animated both with cravings for raw sex and with desires for interpersonal connection.

We ultimately want to enjoy sexual expression as part of an abundant life of abiding in God's freedom, love, and wholeness. When aroused and thinking that sex is all there is, we also want it right now. As such, sex can be both fulfilling and overpowering in our lives.

We are free to do what we want. But lest our freedom lead to shame, bondage, and brokenness, we must balance our liberty with integrity where we hold freedom, love, and wholeness together in sexual expression. Honoring who we are as beloved children of God and our call to enjoy and extend love, consider how you intend to live with sexual integrity—that is, how you intend to be honest about and hold together all your parts in an integrated wholeness. In this exercise, identify your top and bottom lines and how you want to embody your sexuality.

Top line (values I want to honor)

Sexual integrity
(personal practices between my top and bottom lines)

Bottom line (behaviors I intend to avoid)

SPIRITUAL FRIENDSHIPS

Steve

> *Faithful friends are a sturdy shelter;*
> *whoever finds one has found a treasure.*
> *Faithful friends are beyond price;*
> *no amount can balance their worth.*
> *Faithful friends are life-saving medicine.*
> **—Sirach 6:14–16**

Many men long for deeper relationships. One practice to consider is having a spiritual friend—that is, a companion to walk with you along your spiritual journey. In a spiritual friendship, you offer each other mutual encouragement, support, and direction. And together you pay attention to God's presence and leading in your lives.

This kind of friendship involves an intentional practice of meeting regularly—say, over lunch or coffee monthly or every other week. You discuss concerns and joys of your life, talk about your aspirations and questions, and perhaps pray for each other.

To find such a friend, think of someone who can be a companion with you on your spiritual journey. Whom are you drawn to? Whom do you connect with? Who gets you? This may or may not be someone who shares your particular faith. Some people benefit from having a spiritual friend from another faith tradition and find it to be mutually enriching. After thinking of someone, discuss your interest with that person to see whether you might be drawn to each other. If so, explore this practice together for a period and see what happens.

To get started, establish common understandings about what you are seeking, how often you will meet, when and where you will meet, confidentiality, and at what point you will review your practice. In your next meeting, you could share your spiritual journeys and explore some of the themes and questions that emerge for you.

When you meet, you might begin and end by pausing in silence or offering a prayer. Take turns sharing and listening together. Speak from the heart and listen from the heart. To create a safe space for deep sharing, uphold confidentiality and honor the sacred trust between you. Be vulnerable in sharing personal experiences, and allow this to draw you closer. Listen with empathy and without judgment as a way to show respect.

Consider the following subjects:

- Spiritual pilgrimage
- Experience of God
- Images of God
- Spiritual practices
- Relationships with others
- Areas for spiritual growth
- Questions about faith and life

You might consider using the Bible or another book, but be careful that this doesn't distract from sharing your lived experience. It's easy to talk about "it"—a book, ideas, and so on—and not share about yourself.

⚯ FOR CONVERSATION

1. For what are you grateful? How might God be in this?
2. Where are signs of God's presence in your life?
3. How have you received or extended love recently, and what was this like?
4. What has been painful or troubling for you?
5. What struggles are you experiencing? How does God seem near or far in this?
6. What or who helped you become aware of God's presence?
7. What may be blocking your awareness of God?
8. What is stirring within you or getting your attention?
9. What might God want you to know or do?
10. What questions are you wondering about?

Let us consider how to provoke one another to love and good deeds,
not neglecting to meet together . . .
but encouraging one another.
—Hebrews 10:24–25

Recommended resources for spiritual friends
Dorothy Devers, *Faithful Friendship* (Forward Movement, 1986)
Wendy Miller, *Learning to Listen: A Guide for Spiritual Friends* (Upper Room, 1993)
Barry Woodbridge, *A Guidebook for Spiritual Friends* (Upper Room, 1985)

TENDING OUR WOUNDS

Steve

We are wounded men. One of several biblical terms for "man" is the Hebrew word *enosh*—for man in his weakness and woundedness.

Life involves suffering. We are wounded by painful experiences with family, intimate relationships, authority figures, violence, poverty, oppression, addictions, or other hardships.

Where wounded, we need healing for our good and for those around us. As Richard Rohr asserts, what we don't transform, we transmit. Because hurt people, hurt people. Wounded men wound others, projecting their pain onto those around them.

While some men have been wounded by their mothers, Rohr notes that the most common pain men experience is a father wound or father hunger, leaving most men with a huge, aching hole inside them. This is a source not only of great personal pain but also of our social problems as men act out their fear, pain, and anger. Healing this wound can lead to tremendous social reforms.

Patrick Arnold observes:

> Few of us grow up without a father-wound of some kind, and the type inflicted on Ishmael—father neglect—is extremely common today. Every boy needs to relate to a father who will give him a permanent sense of security, a psychic safe-place of sureness and strength that tells him that he belongs, that he is wanted, and that he will make it with a little work. Every boy needs to know that his father is on his side, pulling for him, giving him paternal energy so that whatever he does, he knows he can succeed. If the boy does not receive such assurance from his father, he cannot recreate a firm psychic center within himself, and he is left with a terrible lack of self-esteem and confidence . . . [, and] where psychic holes develop, demons rush in.[1]

Recognizing this wound is not to blame or judge those who have hurt us.

Our goal is not to pass judgment but to reach understanding for our healing and growth with a spirit of compassion.

SEVEN STEPS FOR THE PROCESS OF HEALING

1. Name the wound and its source.
2. Grieve—feel our pain, sadness, and anger.
3. Bring this to God (and others) so it may become a sacred wound.
4. Receive the gifts from our wound.
5. Forgive—let go of our pain, anger, and demands.
6. Embrace our parents and others with understanding and grace.
7. Extend the love we wish we had received.

Remember: What we don't transform, we transmit.

FOR REFLECTION AND CONVERSATION

1. How have I been wounded?
2. How have I hurt or wounded others?
3. To what extend has there been healing and reconciliation?
4. What do I need to forgive or do to make amends?
5. What gifts from my experience do I want to embrace?

NOTES

Introduction

1 For references to appreciative inquiry and spiral dynamics as models for social change, see the sources cited in the introduction of the Social Practices section of this book.

2 Reinhold Niebuhr, *Leaves from the Notebook of a Tamed Cynic* (Westminster, 1990), 75.

3 Patrick Arnold, *Wildmen, Warriors, and Kings: Masculine Spirituality and the Bible* (Crossroad, 1991), 1.

4 Martin Luther King Jr., *A Testament of Hope: The Essential Writings and Speeches*, ed. James M. Washington (HarperOne, 2003), 247.

5 Martin Luther King Jr., *Strength to Love* (Beacon, 2019), 26–27.

6 King Jr., 47.

7 King Jr., Nobel Peace Prize acceptance speech, University of Oslo, December 10, 1964, https://www.nobelprize.org/prizes/peace/1964/king/acceptance-speech/.

8 John Lewis, *Walking with the Wind: A Memoir of the Movement* (Simon & Schuster, 2015), 77.

9 Lewis, 78.

Section 1: Male Formation

1 The Hebrew word *'adam* most frequently refers to humanity collectively with both males and females. Occasionally, *'adam* refers to the male as distinct from the female. In Genesis 1:26–27 and 2:7, *'adam* is used in the collective sense of human creature or humankind. See Eugene F. Roop, *Genesis*, Believers Church Bible Commentary (Herald Press, 1987), 39, 311; and Dorothy Yoder Nyce, "Human Creation Accounts in Genesis 1–3," *Anabaptist Witness* 7, no. 1 (May 2020): 61–73.

2 When processing difficult experiences, many people find assistance helpful, so we suggest counseling for this.

3 Richard Rohr, "Transforming Pain," Center for Action and Contemplation, October 17, 2018, https://cac.org/transforming-pain-2018-10-17/.

4 *Confession of Faith in a Mennonite Perspective* (Herald Press, 1995), 10.

5 See Proverbs, Wisdom, and Sirach in biblical wisdom literature for descriptions of Sophia and her works.

6 Henri J. M. Nouwen, *The Return of the Prodigal Son: A Story of Homecoming* (Doubleday, 1992), 36.

7 Nouwen, 5.

8 A. W. Tozer, *The Knowledge of the Holy: The Attributes of God: Their Meaning in the Christian Life* (Harper, 2009), 1.

9 Brennan Manning, interview, *The Wittenberg Door* (October–November 1986).

10 Mennonite Church, *Confession of Faith*, 10.

11 John Oxenham, "In Christ There Is No East or West," in *Bees in Amber: A Little Book of Thoughtful Verse*, 1913. See *Voices Together 390* (Herald Press, 2020).

12 Thomas R. Yoder Neufeld, "Men Reading the Bible," in *Peaceful at Heart: Anabaptist Reflections on Healthy Masculinity*, ed. Don Neufeld and Steve Thomas (Resource Publications, 2019), 136. For more, see David Augsburger, "Men, Masculinity, and Discipleship," in *Peaceful at Heart*, 142–57.

13 Richard Rohr, "Abstract to Personal," The Cosmic Christ, Center for Action and Contemplation, October 26, 2016, https://cac.org/abstract-to-personal -2016-10-26/. For more, see Rohr, *The Universal Christ: How a Forgotten Reality Can Change Everything We See, Hope For, and Believe* (Society for Promoting Christian Knowledge, 2019).

14 *Confession of Faith*, 18.

15 Steven Charleston, *Ladder to the Light: An Indigenous Elder's Meditations on Hope and Courage* (Broadleaf, 2021), 9.

16 Harris J. Loewen, "New Earth, Heavens New," in Assembly Songs (Hope Publishing, 1983). See *Voices Together 377* (Herald Press, 2020).

17 Noel Moules, *Fingerprints of Fire . . . Footprints of Peace: A Spiritual Manifesto from a Jesus Perspective* (Circle Books, 2012), 9.

18 John Dear, *The Nonviolent Life* (Pace e Bene, 2005), 15–16.

19 It's important to distinguish guilt over wrong behavior from shame that stems from a sense of unworthiness. For more on this, see "Shame" in the Personal Challenges section of this book.

20 Henri J. M. Nouwen, *The Inner Voice of Love: A Journey from Anguish to Freedom* (Doubleday, 1998), 52.

21 Henri J. M. Nouwen, *Life of the Beloved: Spiritual Living in a Secular World* (Crossroad, 2002), 43.

22 Joe Ehrmann, "The 3 Scariest Words a Boy Can Hear," *All Things Considered*, July 14, 2014, 7:25, https://www.npr.org/2014/07/14/330183987/the-3-scariest -words-a-boy-can-hear; Joe Ehrmann, "Being a Man," October 19, 2013, TED video, 3:44, https://www.youtube.com/watch?v=uKmRxkaVZaI.

23 Related terms and definitions describe other important factors concerning gender. *Cisgender* "refers to people whose sex assigned at birth is aligned with their gender identity." *Gender bias* "refers to beliefs and attitudes that involve stereotypes or preconceived ideas about the roles, abilities, and characteristics of males and females that may contain significant distortions and inaccuracies." *Gender role strain* refers to "a psychological situation in which gender role demands have negative consequences on the individual or others." *Gender role conflict* refers to "problems resulting from adherence to 'rigid, sexist, or restrictive gender roles.'" American Psychological Association, *APA Guidelines for Psychological Practice with Boys and Men*, August 2018, 2, https://www.apa.org/about/policy/ boys-men-practice-guidelines.pdf.

24 Antonio Ramírez de León states that while some aspects of culture are external, much of culture is internal, "where certain beliefs, mythologies, attitudes, values, and patterns of behavior and thoughts are born." These internal aspects are

learned implicitly and, in many people, remain in the unconscious. "Therefore, any healthy spirituality, whether male or female, should bring all this subconscious material into consciousness." *The Man: Reflections on Male Spirituality and Identity* (Liguori, 2014), 63.

25 R. W. Connell, *Masculinities*, 2nd ed. (University of California Press, 2005).

26 Jamie Pitts, "Masculinities: Interdisciplinary Orientations," in *Peaceful at Heart*, 27.

27 On the so-called Man Box, see Paul Kivel, "The Act-Like-a-Man Box," in *Men's Lives*, ed. Michael S. Kimmel and Michael A. Messner (Allyn & Bacon, 2009), 83–85; Mark Greene, *The Little #MeToo Book for Men* (ThinkPlay, 2018); and Tony Porter, *Breaking Out of the "Man Box": The Next Generation of Manhood* (Skyhorse, 2020). Or view Porter's TED Talk, "A Call to Men," December 10, 2010, TED video, 11:45, https://youtu.be/td1PbsV6B80?t=1. For Man Box culture among young males, see Brian Heilman, Gary Barker, and Alexander Harrison, *The Man Box: A Study on Being a Young Man in the US, UK, and Mexico* (Promundo and Unilever, 2017), https://www.equimundo.org/resources/man-box-study-young-man-us-uk-mexico/.

28 The American Psychological Association reports that "traditional masculinity ideology has been shown to limit males' psychological development, constrain their behavior, result in gender role strain and gender role conflict and negatively influence mental health and physical health." *Practice with Boys and Men*, 3. The World Health Organization reports that in most parts of the world, while men enjoy more opportunities, privileges, and power than women, the health of boys and men continues to be substantially worse than among girls and women. At least some of the factors involve behavior and risks rooted in patterns of masculinity. Peter Baker et al., "The Men's Health Gap: Men Must Be Included in the Global Health Equity Agenda," *Bulletin of the World Health Organization* 92, no. 8 (August 1, 2014): 618–20, http://dx.doi.org/10.2471/BLT.13.132795.

29 Perry B. Yoder, *Shalom: The Bible's Word for Salvation, Justice, and Peace* (Wipf & Stock, 2017).

30 Table scripture references:
  a. Evident in the Jewish festivals, feasts, and celebrations; Nehemiah 8:10; 9:36; Psalm 16:11; Ecclesiastes 3:12–3; 5:18–19; 8:5, 9:7–9; Isaiah 65:21–22; John 15:11; 17:13; Ephesians 1:3–12.
  b. Matthew 28:18–20; Mark 16:15; John 15:16; Acts 1:8.
  c. John 10:10; 15:1–11.
  d. Genesis 2; Exodus 3:8; Deuteronomy 8:7–10; 26:9; 1 Chronicles 29:20–22; Nehemiah 8:8–10; Ezekiel 34:25–30; Psalm 23:5–6; Matthew 22:2; John 2:1–11; 6:11–13; 10:10; Revelation 19–22.
  e. Exodus 3:7–10; Deuteronomy 26:5–9; John 8:32, 36; Acts 13:38–39; Romans 6; Galatians 5:11; James 1:25; 2:12.
  f. Matthew 22:37–40; John 13:34–35; 15:9–10, 17; Romans 13:8; James 2:8.
  g. Isaiah 2:2–4; 11:6–9; Ezekiel 34:25–30; John 14:25–27; Romans 5:1–11; 14:17; Ephesians 2:14–18.

31 See Don Neufeld, "Confined to Caricature: Moving Past the Stereotypes of Masculinity That Harm Both Men and Women," *Mutuality*, March 5, 2014, https://www.cbeinternational.org/resource/confined-caricature/; TonyPorter's

powerful Ted Talk "A Call to Men"; and Jesuit Social Services, "The Man Box: The Men's Project," October 15, 2018, video, 2:19, https://www.youtube.com/watch?v=KdRrjCOqzZY.

32 More than following Jesus in behavior is *abiding in* Christ in union with him. Much of the Anabaptist tradition emphasizes this outer dimension, with less emphasis on the inner dimension of our life "in Christ"—a key phrase occurring 26 times in John's writings and 216 times in Paul's. Our spiritual life is rooted at a deeper level in the interior of our lives, tending our connection with "Christ who lives in me" (Galatians 2:20).

33 Quoted in Stephen K. Hatch, *Wilderness Mysticism: A Contemplative Christian Tradition* (Lulu, 2018), 12.

34 Terry Real, *I Don't Want to Talk about It: Overcoming the Secret Legacy of Male Depression* (Scribner, 1997), 23, 24. See also Charlie Donaldson and Randy Flood, *Mascupathy: Understanding and Healing the Malaise of American Manhood* (Institute for the Prevention and Treatment of Mascupathy, 2014).

35 On archetypes in the Bible, see Patrick Arnold, *Wildmen, Warriors, and Kings: Masculine Spirituality and the Bible* (Crossroad, 1991). For psychological and mythopoetic perspectives, see Robert Moore and Douglas Gillette, *King, Warrior, Magician, Lover: Rediscovering the Archetypes of the Mature Masculine* (HarperCollins, 1991), and their in-depth treatments of each of these main archetypes.

Section 2: Human Needs

1 Vern Neufeld Redekop, *From Violence to Blessing: How an Understanding of a Deep-Rooted Conflict Can Open Paths to Reconciliation* (Novalis, 2002). We also used this material in chapter 1 of our book *Peaceful at Heart: Reflections on Healthy Masculinity* (Resource Publications, 2019).

Section 3: Personal Challenges

1 Parker Palmer, "Heartbreak, Violence, and Hope for New Life," On Being, April 30, 2015, https://onbeing.org/blog/heartbreak-violence-and-hope-for-new-life/. Emphasis in the original.

2 Palmer.

3 Palmer.

4 Brené Brown, *Daring Greatly: How the Courage to Be Vulnerable Transforms the Way We Live, Love, Parent, and Lead* (Gotham, 2021), 69.

5 Brown, 92.

6 Stevenson, *Just Mercy*, 290.

7 Gareth Brandt, *Under Construction: Reframing Men's Spirituality* (Herald Press, 2009), 58.

8 Norman P. Grubb, *Yes, I Am* (Zerubbabel, 2000), 74. Emphasis in the original.

9 Brown, *Daring Greatly*, 12.

10 Brown, 34.

11 The inspiration for this approach of working with men has come from Alan Jenkins, *Becoming Ethical: A Parallel, Political Journey with Men Who Have Abused* (Russell House, 2009).

12 Once prejudices are established in our systems, discrimination, privilege, and oppression can become the norm and happen automatically whether or not we are aware of it. For how prejudice, discrimination, power, privilege, and oppression operate in social systems, see Isabel Wilkerson, *Caste: The Origins of Our Discontent* (Random House, 2020); Allan G. Johnson, *Privilege, Power, and Difference* (McGraw-Hill, 2006); and Allan G. Johnson, *The Gender Knot: Unraveling Our Patriarchal Legacy* (Temple University Press, 2014). To examine male privilege, see, e.g., Barry Deutsch, "The Male Privilege Checklist," in *Men's Lives*, ed. Michael S. Kimmel and Michael A. Messner (Allyn & Bacon, 2009), 14–16.

Section 4: Sexual Wholeness

1 Jeffrey Kluger, "Love, Sex, and Health: Biology: The Power of Love," *Time*, January 19, 2004.

2 In biological terms, human beings have both a brain stem with more primitive drives and a neocortex for complex functioning to express who we are. Brain science explains the difference between lower and more evolved forms of sexual interaction. Scientists state that the drive for sex lies in the basal ganglia. This is the primitive control center for the four primary animal instincts: fleeing, fighting, feeding, and reproducing. Psychiatrist and neuroscientist Daniel Amen describes what happens when we are engaged in sex as human beings with a more evolved brain. The hormone oxytocin is released during sex, which creates a pair bond with neurochemical attachment. The person we become bonded to lives in the emotional or limbic centers of our brains and is embedded in our memory circuits. With the entanglement of subatomic particles, bonded humans become as one unit, "one flesh." Amen states that "being inside another person's body, becoming one with him or her, allows for the exchange not only of bodily fluids, but also of energy forces, thoughts, and intentions." As such, "sexual union can be a spiritual experience." *Sex on the Brain: 12 Lessons to Enhance Your Love Life* (Three Rivers, 2008), 144.

3 Christian tradition has held that the intention is for sex to be expressed in a lifelong, loving covenant relationship. While this prescription is increasingly dismissed by individuals in the name of freedom, when practiced it provides a permanent, secure, and exclusive setting for a couple to most fully enjoy sex with greater freedom, intimacy, and love, and for many couples, the possibility of becoming parents. In *Sex, Gender, and Christian Ethics* (Cambridge University Press, 1996), Lisa Sowle Cahill writes, "Human flourishing, as sexually embodied, depends on the realization of the *equality of the sexes*, male and female; and, in their sexual union on the further values of *reproduction, pleasure, and intimacy*. The institutions gender, marriage, and family should . . . enhance these values" (110, emphasis in the original). She goes on to write that "the task of a Christian social ethic of sex is to imbue sexual and reproductive behavior with the qualities of respect, empathy, reciprocity, and mutual fidelity which would allow sexual and parental love to be transforming agents in society in general" (119).

4 James Nelson writes that

> sexuality is that basic *eros* of our humanness—urging, pulling, luring, driving us out of loneliness into communion. . . . Indeed, the word "sexuality" itself comes from the Latin *secare*, meaning "to cut or divide." The word suggests our appetite for a wholeness that can be appeased only through intimacy. Sexuality thus is a deep human energy driving us toward bonding and compassion, and without it life would be cold and metallic. Even in its distorted and destructive expressions, sexuality betrays this fundamental longing. It is God-given for no less than that. (*The Intimate Connection: Male Sexuality, Masculine Spirituality* [Westminster/John Knox, 1988], 26)

5 Ronald Rolheiser, *The Holy Longing: The Search for a Christian Spirituality* (Doubleday, 1999), 195–96.

6 Rolheiser, 194–95.

7 The church thought that artist Marcantonio Raimondi went too far in the sixteenth century with *I Modi* (*The Ways*), also known as *The Sixteen Pleasures*, a famous collection of sexual positions. The Catholic Church condemned and destroyed the original images and imprisoned Raimondi. Eric Berkowitz, *Sex and Punishment: Four Thousand Years of Judging Desire* (Counterpoint, 2013), 195.

8 Richard Rohr, *From Wild Man to Wise Man: Reflections on Male Spirituality* (St. Anthony Messenger, 2005), 120–21.

9 Rohr, 122. James Nelson states that we tend to undervalue the soft penis and overvalue the erect phallus—that in our patriarchal culture we have been taught "bigger is better. . . hardness is superior to softness . . . upness is better than downness. In a 'man's world,' small, soft, and down pale beside big, hard, and up." *Intimate Connection*, 95. Nelson also offers reflections on the phallus and the penis. For treatment on the phallus from a mythopoetic perspective, see Robert Moore and Douglas Gillette, *The Lover Within: Accessing the Lover in the Male Psyche* (William Morrow, 1993).

10 David Boshart, *Sex and Faith: Celebrating God's Gifts* (Faith & Life Resources, 2003), 35.

11 Song of Songs 7:6–9; 4:12–13; 4:16; 5:1 (RSV).

12 In *The Lover Within*, Moore and Gillette describe the connection that ancient Greek philosophers made between sexuality and spirituality with their view of *erōs*:

> According to Plato, eros is the yearning of the human soul for union with the Divine. Humankind's essence is spiritual and belongs to the world of light beyond time and space. . . . Eros begins when the soul, stimulated by sensuous or sexual pleasure, desires union with the remembered beauties of the Garden of Delight. The soul gradually rises heavenward as it comes to realize that the union it longs for cannot be attained in this world. Thus eros, originally sensual and sexual in nature, becomes a profoundly spiritualizing drive. (84)

That this was also held by some Jewish thinkers is evident with Philo of Alexandria, the great Jewish scholar (30 BC–AD 40). He translated the central command of Judaism—to love God with all one's heart, and mind, and strength—not with *agapē* but with *erōs*.

13 C. S. Lewis, *The Four Loves* (Harcourt, 1960), 134.

14 The book of Maccabees is in the Apocrypha, which is found in most, but not all, Bibles.

15 Rolheiser writes that "spirituality is about what we do with the fire inside of us, about how we channel our eros. And how we do channel it, the disciplines and habits we choose to live by, will either lead to a greater integration or disintegration within our bodies, minds, and souls, and to a greater integration or disintegration in the way we are related to God, others, and the cosmic world." *Holy Longing*, 11.

16 The root of the word *integrity* is instructive, especially for its second meaning. It comes from the Latin word *integritas*, which is from *integer*, for "intact." *Integration* is also from this Latin root, which is also suggestive.

17 Rohr, *From Wild Man to Wise Man*, 75.

18 Keith Miller, *Habitation of Dragons* (Word, 1983), 148–50. Miller notes that Thomas à Kempis pointed out in his spiritual classic *The Imitation of Christ* that the only time to stop temptation is at the first point of recognition. If one begins to argue and engage in a hand-to-hand combat, temptation almost always wins the day.

19 Mary Pipher, *Reviving Ophelia: Saving the Selves of Adolescent Girls* (Ballantine, 1994), 12.

20 Sexual orientation refers to an inherent, enduring emotional, physical, or sexual attraction to other people. Sexual orientation ranges from exclusive homosexuality to exclusive heterosexuality and includes various forms of bisexuality.

21 As it is often used, in this writing the term *gay* includes those who are lesbian or bisexual.

22 Justin Lee, *Torn: Rescuing the Gospel from the Gays-vs.-Christians Debate* (Jericho, 2012), 166.

23 Our sexual orientation is not something within our control. Trying to change this through reparative or conversion therapy is not only ineffective but also harmful. See American Psychiatric Association, "Position Statement on Issues Related to Homosexuality," APA Official Actions, July 2000, https://www .psychiatry.org/File%20Library/About-APA/Organization-Documents-Policies/ Policies/Position-2013-Homosexuality.pdf; American Medical Association, "LGBTQ Change Efforts (So-Called 'Conversion Therapy')," accessed May 14, 2021, https://www.ama-assn.org/system/files/2019-12/conversion-therapy-issue -brief.pdf; and American Psychological Association, "Sexual Orientation and Homosexuality," created 2008, https://www.apa.org/topics/lgbtq/orientation.

24 Pieter Niemeyer, "A Gay Man," in *Peaceful at Heart: Anabaptist Reflections on Healthy Masculinity*, ed. Don Neufeld and Steve Thomas (Resource Publications, 2019), 112, 120. For definitions of transgender and queer, see "Identities" later in this section on sexual wholeness.

25 Niemeyer, 113.

26 For resources addressing this question from various perspectives, see books under "Sexuality" in "Resources for Further Discussion and Action" at bit.ly/ LivingThatMatters.

27 Based on this text, Mennonite Church USA in 2015 adopted *Forbearance in*

the Midst of Differences, a wise resolution to hold the church together. Refer to this important statement for agreeing and disagreeing in love and remaining together despite our differences.

28 For introductory resources on gender identity, see American Psychological Association, "Sexual Orientation and Gender Identity," created 2011, https://www.apa.org/topics/sexual-orientation. For a more comprehensive resource, see American Psychological Association, *APA Guidelines for Psychological Practice with Boys and Men*, August 2018, https://www.apa.org/about/policy/boys-men-practice-guidelines.pdf.

To understand the complexities around sexual indentities, consider these terms:

Gender identity: One's self-concept as a female, male, a blend of both, or neither.

Gender expression: External appearance or presentation of one's gender identity through dress and behavior.

Cisgender: Refers to individuals whose gender identity aligns with their assigned sex at birth.

Transgender: Refers to people whose gender identity or expression varies from social expectations based on one's assigned sex at birth.

Queer: Refers to people who identify as neither male nor female, or as a combination of genders, or as beyond any gender—or whose sexual orientation does not conform to social norms.

Intersex: Refers to individuals born with sex chromosomes, hormones, or reproductive systems that do not fit typical boxes for male or female bodies.

29 Niemeyer, "A Gay Man," 119. See pages 116–17 for how Christian faith challenges binary models. For resources addressing this issue from various Christian perspectives, see books under "Sexuality" in "Resources for Further Discussion and Action" at bit.ly/LivingThatMatters.

30 Niemeyer, 117.

31 Consider the words from traditional wedding vows: "forsaking all others" and "faithful to him/her as long as we both shall live."

32 See the discussion regarding "preferred self" in "Values" in the Male Formation section in this book.

33 See also "Compulsions" in the Personal Challenges section.

Section 5: Social Practices

1 Perry B. Yoder, *Shalom: The Bible's Word for Salvation, Justice, and Peace* (Wipf & Stock, 2017), 22.

2 On appreciative inquiry for promoting social change, see David L. Cooperrider, Diana K. Whitney, and Jacqueline M. Stavros, *The Appreciative Inquiry Handbook: For Leaders of Change*, 2nd ed. (Berrett-Koehler, 2008); Sarah Lewis, *Positive Psychology and Change: How Leadership, Collaboration, and Appreciative Inquiry Create Transformational Results* (Wiley-Blackwell, 2016). For another approach that appeals to values in social systems, see Don Edward Beck and Christopher C. Cowen, *Spiral Dynamics: Mastering Values, Leadership, and Change* (Blackwell, 2006); Michael C. Armour and Don Browning, *Systems-*

Sensitive Leadership: Empowering Diversity without Polarizing the Church (College, 1995).

3 Cornel West, speech, 2011, Howard University, Washington, DC.

4 See also "Mutuality" later in this section.

5 William R. White, *Stories for Telling: A Treasury for Christian Storytellers* (Augsburg, 1986), 30.

6 Henri J. M. Nouwen, Donald P. McNeill, and Douglas A. Morrison, *Compassion: A Reflection on the Christian Life* (Image, 2006), 3–4.

7 Nouwen, McNeill, and Morrison, 124.

8 George Orwell, *Animal Farm* (Harcourt, Brace, 1946).

9 See John 13:34; Romans 12:10, 16; 14:19; 15:5, 7, 14; 16:16; 1 Corinthians 12:25; Galatians 5:13; 6:2; Ephesians 4:2, 15, 25, 32; 5:19, 21; Philippians 2:3, 4; Colossians 3:13, 16; 1 Thessalonians 4:18; 5:11; Hebrews 3:13; 10:24; 1 Peter 4:9; 5:5; James 5:16.

10 See the section "Human Needs." Our ability as men to know ourselves as needy opens us to receive what others offer to us in a mutually loving relationship.

11 *Oxford English and Spanish Dictionary*, s.v. "freedom," https://www.lexico.com/definition/freedom.

12 Brian Zahnd, in *Sinners in the Hands of a Loving God: The Scandalous Truth of the Very Good News* (Waterbrook, 2017), thoroughly deconstructs traditional pictures of God as angry, violent, and retributive. See also Gregory Boyd, *Is God to Blame? Beyond Pat Answers to the Problem of Suffering* (InterVarsity, 2003); Thomas J. Oord, *God Can't! How to Believe in God and Love after Tragedy, Abuse, or Other Evils* (SacraSage, 2019).

13 Dallas Willard, *The Divine Conspiracy: Rediscovering Our Hidden Life in God* (HarperCollins, 1998), 230.

14 For further insight, see Isabel Wilkerson, *Caste: The Origins of Our Discontent* (Random House, 2020).

15 For a fuller development of the roots and impacts of inequality, see Carolyn Holderread Heggen, *Sexual Abuse in Christian Homes and Churches* (Herald Press, 1993); Wilkerson, *Caste*; and Kristin Kobes Du Mez, *Jesus and John Wayne: How White Evangelicals Corrupted a Faith and Fractured a Nation* (Liveright, 2020).

16 Noel Moules, *Fingerprints of Fire . . . Footprints of Peace: A Spiritual Manifesto from a Jesus Perspective* (Circle Books, 2012), 48.

17 Likewise, the Greek word *dikaiosune*, which Jesus frequently used, can be translated in terms of "righteousness" or "justice." Unfortunately, righteousness has too often been used to translate *dikaiosune* and spiritualized to the point where it has lost much of its practical meaning of embodying justice. We would do better to translate *tzedakah* and *dikaiosune* as "justice" to express what God calls for.

18 On white supremacy as a basis for racial injustice, see "Dismantling Racism Works Web Workbook," dRworksBook, accessed September 6, 2022, https://www.dismantlingracism.org/. On white supremacy in the Doctrine of Discovery and the US Constitution, and the injustices of patriarchy, racism, and the displacement of Native Americans, see Mark Charles, "The Truth Behind 'We the

People'—The Three Most Misunderstood Words in US History," January 24, 2019, TEDxTysons video, 17:44, https://youtu.be/HOktqY5wY4A?t=6. For a checklist on white privilege, see Peggy McIntosh, "White Privilege: Unpacking the Invisible Knapsack," *Peace and Freedom Magazine* (July/August 1989): 10–12, available at https://nationalseedproject.org/Key-SEED-Texts/white -privilege-unpacking-the-invisible-knapsack.

19 Quoted in Robert McAfee Brown, *Unexpected News: Reading the Bible with Third World Eyes* (Westminster, 1984), 19.

20 Elie Wiesel, Nobel Peace Prize acceptance speech, Oslo, Sweden, December 10, 1986, https://eliewieselfoundation.org/about-elie-wiesel/nobel-prize-speech/.

21 Omid Safi, "Justice Is Love, Embodied," On Being Project, March 24, 2016, https://onbeing.org/blog/justice-is-love-embodied/.

22 John Lewis, "Together, You Can Redeem the Soul of Our Nation," *New York Times*, July 30, 2020, https://www.nytimes.com/2020/07/30/opinion/john-lewis -civil-rights-america.html.

23 For concise resources on justice, see the following publications in the Little Books of Justice and Peacebuilding Series: Fania E. Davis, *The Little Book of Race and Restorative Justice: Black Lives, Healing, and US Social Transformation* (Good Books, 2019); Thomas Norman DeWolf and Jodie Geddes, *The Little Book of Racial Healing: Coming to the Table for Truth-Telling, Liberation, and Transformation* (Good Books, 2019); Chris Marshall, *The Little Book of Biblical Justice: A Fresh Approach to the Bible's Teaching on Justice* (Good Books, 2005).

24 See note 20.

25 Robin DiAngelo, *White Fragility: Why It's So Hard for White People to Talk about Racism* (Beacon, 2018), viii.

26 Walter Brueggemann, *Tenacious Solidarity: Biblical Provocations on Race, Religion, Climate, and the Economy*, ed. Davis Hankins (Fortress, 2018), 117.

27 Brueggemann, 135. See also Paul Kivel, "The Doctrine of Discovery, Manifest Destiny, and American Exceptionalism," Challenging Christian Hegemony, July 21, 2015, https://christianhegemony.org/2015/07.

28 See "Identity" in the Male Formation section of this book.

29 World Commission on Environment and Development, *Our Common Future* (Oxford University Press, 1987).

30 Mark A. Benedict and Edward T. McMahon, *Green Infrastructure: Linking Landscapes and Communities* (Island, 2006), 200.

31 United Nations, *Planning for the Future*, ch. 2, accessed May 15, 2021, https://sdgs.undp.org/2020-sustainable-consumption/chapter-2.html. For Indigenous wisdom for stewardship, care of the earth, and sustainability, see Robin Wall Kimmerer's description of the honorable harvest in *Braiding Sweetgrass: Indigenous Wisdom, Scientific Knowledge, and the Teaching of Plants* (Milkweed, 2013), 173–201.

32 William J. Manning, *Trees and Global Warming: The Role of Forests in Cooling and Warming the Atmosphere* (Cambridge, 2020), 11–12.

33 FAO and UNEP, *The State of the World's Forests 2020: Forests, Biodiversity and People* (FAO and UNEP, 2020), https://doi.org/10.4060/ca8642en.

34 "UN Report: Nature's Dangerous Decline 'Unprecedented'; Species Extinction

Rates 'Accelerating,'" *Sustainable Development*, May 6, 2019, https://www.un.org/sustainabledevelopment/blog/2019/05/nature-decline-unprecedented-report/.

35 Global Footprint Network, "Footprint Calculator," accessed May 14, 2021, https://www.footprintnetwork.org/resources/footprint-calculator/.

36 Randy Woodley, *Becoming Rooted: One Hundred Days of Reconnecting with Sacred Earth* (Broadleaf, 2022), 137.

37 For a more detailed assessment of your personal ecological footprint, see the EPA's carbon footprint calculator at https://www3.epa.gov/carbon-footprint -calculator/.

38 In Genesis 2:25, in the narrative about the garden, Adam and Eve are described as being "naked and not ashamed." This image of unmasked intimacy offers a vision of what we are truly created for!

39 Clinical counseling with a therapist familiar with men's experiences of trauma and difficulties with vulnerability is an important step for men who are struggling. A couple of important books that might also be helpful are *I Don't Want to Talk about It* by Terry Real and *Daring Greatly* by Brené Brown.

40 For more about this collaborative venture, see Woodland Cultural Centre, "Joint MCC, MDS Project to Promote Healing, Reconciliation with Indigenous Canadians," May 22, 2019, https://woodlandculturalcentre.ca/mennonite-disaster -service-mds-canada-and-mennonite-central-committee-mcc-partner-with -save-the-evidence/.

Section 6: Conflict Tools

1 Stuart Murray, *The Naked Anabaptist: The Bare Essentials of a Radical Faith* (Herald Press, 2015), 46. First published 2010.

2 For a depiction of the visible, hidden, and invisible forms of power and the different spaces and levels of power, see the "powercube" model at PowerCube.net and the work of John Gaventa.

3 See Allan G. Johnson, *Privilege, Power, and Difference* (McGraw-Hill, 2006), on how power works in social relationships; Joyce L. Hocker and William W. Wilmot, *Interpersonal Conflict* (McGraw-Hill Education, 2017), on power in interpersonal conflict; and Walter Wink, *Engaging the Powers: Discernment and Resistance in a World of Domination* (Fortress, 1992), for biblical perspectives on power.

4 On various forms of power, see Rollo May, *Power and Innocence: A Search for the Sources of Violence* (W. W. Norton, 1998). In this classic study, May distinguishes between exploitative, manipulative, competitive, nutrient, and integrative kinds of powers.

5 Martin Luther King Jr., *A Testament of Hope: The Essential Writings and Speeches*, ed. James M. Washington (HarperOne, 2003), 247.

6 For our wholeness and the healing of the world, we must find appropriate ways to wield our power. See Dwight Judy, *Healing the Male Soul: Christianity and the Mythic Journey* (Crossroad, 1992), on claiming and exercising power as a form of agency to be creative as God intended us to be.

7 David Evans, "Trading Manpower for the Power of Love," in *Peaceful at Heart: Anabaptist Reflections on Healthy Masculinity*, ed. Don Neufeld and Steve

Thomas (Resource Publications, 2019), 202. See also John Powell, "Becoming Men of Peace and Reconciliation," in *Peaceful at Heart*, 218–31.

8 On the physiological fight-or-flight response, see Herbert Benson and Eileen M. Stuart, *The Wellness Book: The Comprehensive Guide to Maintaining Health and Treating Stress-Related Illness* (Scribner, 1992), 34. For an in-depth description, refer to Mark Mattson, ed., *Neurobiology of Aggression: Understanding and Preventing Violence* (Humana, 2003).

9 See Wink, *Engaging the Powers*; and *Jesus and Nonviolence: A Third Way* (Fortress, 2003).

10 Kazu Haga has a simple way to remember the third way of nonviolence: rather than fleeing or fighting, we can face aggression. "For most of us, our natural reactions to violence fall into one of three categories: to fight, flight, or freeze. Nonviolence gives us an alternative way of responding: to face. Facing means looking your assailant in the eye, not backing down, not giving into fear, and not reacting in kind." *Healing Resistance: A Radically Different Response to Harm* (Parallax, 2018), 41.

11 Steve Thomas, "Martial Arts as a Model for Nonviolence: Resisting Interpersonal Violence with Assertive Force," *Conrad Grebel Review* 33, no. 1 (Winter 2015): 72–91.

12 List adapted from Wink, *Engaging the Powers*, 175–93. See also Wink, *Jesus and Nonviolence*.

13 Nelson Mandela, *Long Walk to Freedom: The Autobiography of Nelson Mandela* (Back Bay, 1995), 622.

14 Rosa Parks, *Quiet Strength: The Faith, the Hope, and the Heart of a Woman Who Changed a Nation* (Zondervan, 1994), 17.

15 JoAnne Lingle, sermon, First Mennonite Church, Indianapolis, IN, September 28, 2014.

16 For more on this practice, see Benson and Stuart, *Wellness Book*, ch. 4–5, and Benson's other publications on the relaxation response.

17 This is seen in how we refer to men and women when they express anger. When a man expresses anger, he is often called "strong," but when a woman does this she is often referred to using a pejorative term.

18 Anger tells us that something deeper is troubling us; we feel pain, fear, sadness, or something else. If we don't name and address these deeper needs, we may turn to substances or behaviors for momentary relief without addressing the problem. We may also act out in violent ways, seeking to control others or lash out at them. So it's important to be aware of what we feel and to find healthy ways to get what we need. If you don't know what to do with your anger, ask someone for help.

19 Marshall B. Rosenberg, *Nonviolent Communication: A Language of Life* (PuddleDancer, 2003), viii.

20 See Terry Real, "10 Commandments of Time Outs," June 1, 2017, https://terryreal.com/10-commandments-of-time-outs/.

21 As introduced in "Courage" in this book, centering is a helpful practice to manage anger through calming down and controlling reactions with slow, deep breathing. In their (recorded) retreat, Richard Rohr and Thomas Keating suggest

the practice of centering as a means to transform the inner roots of violence within us by allowing God's Spirit to work within and through us to bring about peace. We can focus our minds with an image, word, phrase, or prayer. We can simply repeat a word like *shalom* with our breath, a phrase like "I can control myself" or "precious and strong," or a prayer like "I rest in you, Spirit of Peace." Rohr and Keating, *Healing Our Violence: Through the Journey of Centering Prayer* (St. Anthony Messenger, 2002), audiobook. Thich Nhat Hanh says, "Breathing in, I calm body and mind. Breathing out, I smile." "Being Peace," *Fellowship of Reconciliation* (July–August 1986): 15.

22 For an in-depth resource for paying attention to important messages of difficult emotions, see James Whitehead, *Shadows of the Heart: A Spirituality of the Negative Emotions* (Crossroad, 1994).

23 For more on managing and expressing anger in conflict, see Rosenberg, *Nonviolent Communication* and *The Surprising Purpose of Anger: Beyond Anger Management: Finding the Gift* (PuddleDancer, 2005). For general resources, refer to resources in "Anger" in the Personal Challenges section.

24 Stephen R. Covey, *The 7 Habits of Highly Effective People: Powerful Lessons in Personal Change* (Free Press, 2004), 250.

25 Covey, 277.

26 For a process of compassionate listening, see Rosenberg, *Nonviolent Communication*, 91–127. We refer to Rosenberg's model for nonviolent or compassion communication in the next reflection—"Speaking."

27 On this key point, see Roger Fisher, William Ury, and Bruce Patton, *Getting to Yes: Negotiating Agreement without Giving In* (Penguin, 2011).

28 See Rosenberg, *Nonviolent Communication*, for more on this practical communication process and learning how to identify and express our feelings and needs.

29 See *Style Matters: The Kraybill Conflict Style Inventory* (Riverhouse, 2005) by Ron Kraybill, an early Mennonite pioneer in conflict transformation. His inventory to identify personal styles of response and descriptions for strengthening responses to conflict can be found online at https://www.riverhouseepress.com. People find it helpful to know their style and receive "hot tips" on managing themselves in conflict. A group may want to do this inventory together and then discuss the results.

30 Adapted from the Thomas-Kilman model and course materials from David Augsburger. For more description of these approaches, see *Mediation and Facilitation Training Manual*, 5th ed. (Office on Justice and Peacebuilding of Mennonite Central Committee, 2008), 34–39.

31 Developed by Steve Thomas with Phil Thomas for Peacemakers. For a free PDF of the *EmPower* peace curriculum with this and other models, contact Steve Thomas at SteveForPeace@gmail.com.

Section 7: Life Roles

1 Patrick M. Arnold, in *Wildmen, Warriors, and Kings: Masculine Spirituality and the Bible* (Crossroad, 1991); and Robert Moore and Douglas Gillette, *King, Warrior, Magician, Lover: Rediscovering the Archetypes of the Mature Masculine*

(HarperCollins, 1991), integrate these perspectives and discuss how they are portrayed in the Bible, classic literature, and throughout history.

2 See Richard Rohr, *From Wild Man to Wise Man: Reflections on Male Spirituality* (St. Anthony Messenger, 2005), 12, 65–79; Terry Real, *I Don't Want to Talk about It: Overcoming the Secret Legacy of Male Depression* (Scribner, 1997).

3 John Lee, *Breaking the Mother-Son Dynamic: Resetting the Patterns of a Man's Life and Loves* (Health Communications, 2015), 13.

4 John Lee, *The Flying Boy: Healing the Wounded Man* (Health Communications, 1989), 14.

5 Moore and Gillette, *King, Warrior, Magician, Lover*, 121. For a more exhaustive treatment of this role as an archetype, see Robert Moore and Douglas Gillette, *The Lover Within: Accessing the Lover in the Male Psyche* (William Morrow, 1993).

6 For a deeper dive into the science of love, see Sue Johnston, *Love Sense: The Revolutionary New Science of Romantic Relationships* (Little, Brown, 2013).

7 See also in this book "Mutuality," "Love," and "Equity" (within the Social Practices section) and "Intimacy" (within the Sexual Wholeness section).

8 The biblical text, written in a context that was deeply influenced by a patriarchal world view, largely assumes the role of husbands to be in hierarchical dominance over women and children. Just how *prescriptive* these understandings of men's roles in relationships should be today continues to be significant contention in Christian circles. Should first-century views on human hierarchy that are *descriptive* of human attempts to live faithfully to God in a specific time and space be the pattern for today?

9 It is significant how emphatic Paul is in passages like Ephesians 5 about men loving their wives (vv. 25; 28; 33). His emphasis has sadly been missed, or deliberately overlooked, throughout the years.

10 Paul Kivel, *Boys Will Be Men: Raising Our Sons for Courage, Caring and Community* (New Society, 1999), 1–2.

11 Scott Coltrane, "Fathering: Paradoxes, Contradictions, and Dilemmas," in *Men's Lives*, ed. Michael A. Kimmel and Michael A. Messner (Pearson, 2010), 433. This chapter summarizes studies on the changing roles of fathers through history, various models for fathers, and the effects on child development.

12 Fathering can be fraught with emotional impacts such as postpartum depression in men, loss or deep pain as children die or stray from family hopes, and especially the complexities of custody and access conflicts (including institutional alignments against father involvement and dismissal of the importance of fathers in the family system).

13 For healing the wounds from our parents so we don't wound our children, Sam Keen offers this guidance:

> In our hurt lies the source of our healing. Where you stumble and fall, there you find the treasure. One of men's greatest resources for change is our wound and our longing for the missing father. We can heal ourselves by becoming the kind of fathers we wanted but did not have. . . . Our best map for parenting is outlined like a photographic negative in the shadow side of our psyches. Get in touch with your disappointment, your rage, your grief, your loneliness for the father, the intimate touching family you did not have, and

you will have a blueprint for parenting. Become the father you longed for. We heal ourselves by learning to give our children what we did not receive. (*Fire in the Belly: On Being a Man* [Bantam, 1992], 226)

14 Henri J. M. Nouwen, *Letters to Marc about Jesus* (HarperOne, 2009).

15 In *The Boy Crisis: Why Our Boys Are Struggling and What We Can Do about It* (BenBella, 2018), Warren Farrell develops this idea, stating: "Fatherhood was about your dad trading in the old glint in his eye—what *he* loved to do—for the new glint in his eye: his love for you" (48).

16 For this perspective of leadership, see Walter C. Wright, *Relational Leadership: A Biblical Model for Leadership Service* (Paternoster, 2000).

17 For understanding the visible, hidden, and invisible forms of power and the different spaces and levels of power, see the "powercube" model at https://www.powercube.net; and the work of John Gaventa.

18 Quoted in "The Servant as Leader," Robert K. Greenleaf Center for Servant Leadership, accessed September 6, 2022, https://www.greenleaf.org/what-is-servant-leadership/. For Greenleaf's classic book on this, see *Servant Leadership: A Journey into the Nature of Legitimate Power and Greatness* (Paulist Press, 2002).

19 For an archetype approach to leaders, refer to the king archetype in Arnold, *Wildmen, Warriors, and Kings*; Moore and Gillette, *King, Warrior, Magician, Lover*; and Robert Moore and Douglas Gillette, *The King Within: Accessing the King within the Male Psyche* (Exploration, 2007).

20 Gabe Huck, ed., *The Psalter: A Faithful and Inclusive Rendering from the Hebrew into Contemporary English Poetry, Intended Primarily for Communal Song and Recitation* (Liturgy Training, 1995).

21 Walter Brueggemann, in *Genesis* (John Knox, 1982), states:

The "dominion" here mandated is with reference to the animals. The dominance is that of a shepherd who cares for, tends, and feeds the animals. Thus the task of "dominion" does not have to do with exploitation and abuse. It has to do with securing the well-being of every other creature and bringing the promise of each to full fruition. . . .

Moreover, a Christian understanding of dominion must be discerned in the way of Jesus of Nazareth (cf. Mark 10:43–44). The one who rules is the one who serves. Lordship means servanthood. It is the task of the shepherd not to control but to lay down his life for the sheep (John 10:11). The human person is ordained over the remainder of creation but for its profit, well-being, and enhancement. The role of the human person is to see to it that the creation becomes fully the creation willed by God. (32–33)

This is connected to humankind's vocation in Genesis 2:15 (NABRE) to "cultivate and care for" the garden. Brueggemann interprets this to mean to care for and tend the earth as a gardener or a shepherd. "From the beginning, the human creature is called, given a vocation, and expected to share in God's work" (46).

22 Aldo Leopold, *A Sand County Almanac: With Essays on Conservation* (Oxford, 2001), 21. Leopold called for a land ethic "that enlarges the boundaries of the community to include soils, waters, plants, and animals, or collectively: the land." This "land ethic changes the role of *Homo sapiens* from conqueror of the

land-community to plain member and citizen of it. It implies respect for his fellow-members and also respect for the community as such" (171).

23 H. Paul Santmire translates this phrase as "to serve (*abad*) the land and protect (*samar*) it." "Partnership with Nature According to the Scriptures: Beyond the Theology of Stewardship," *Christian Scholar's Review* 32, no. 4 (Summer 2003): 402. He suggests that our call is not so much to be stewards of the earth as to be partners with nature, with emphasis on our relationship with the earth.

24 Robin Wall Kimmerer, *Braiding Sweetgrass: Indigenous Wisdom, Scientific Knowledge, and the Teaching of Plants* (Milkweed, 2013), 376.

25 Arnold, *Wildmen, Warriors, and Kings*, 32. For an in-depth treatment of the warrior, see Robert Moore and Douglas Gillette, *The Warrior Within: Accessing the Knight in the Male Psyche* (William Morrow, 1992). For a short treatment, refer to Gordon Dalbey, *Healing the Masculine Soul: How God Restores Men to Real Manhood* (W Publishing, 2003), 113–26.

26 Rohr writes, "Warriors are not going to stop fascinating young boys because feminist mothers don't like it or pacifists rail against it. Like most of the great world religions, we just have to discover the meaning of the spiritual warrior." *From Wild Man to Wise Man*, 149. Along with Rohr, who's committed to the way of nonviolence, I believe it's a matter of rightly forming and engaging the warrior.

27 Steve Thomas, "Martial Arts as a Model for Nonviolence: Resisting Interpersonal Violence with Assertive Force," *Conrad Grebel Review* 33, no. 1 (Winter): 72–91. For training peaceful warriors, you may request free PDFs of my *EmPower Peacemakers* instructor and student manuals by contacting me at SteveT@ MennoniteMen.org or SteveForPeace@gmail.com.

28 Morihei Ueshiba, *The Art of Peace: Teachings of the Founder of Aikido*, trans. and ed. John Stevens (Shambhala, 1992).

29 Shifts occur in the Old Testament from God fighting *for* Israel to Israel fighting *with* God to Israel fighting *for* God. For a treatment of this, see "The Biblical Call to Nonviolence and Peace" at bit.ly/LivingThatMatters; and Milliard Lind, *Yahweh Is a Warrior: The Theology of Warfare in Ancient Israel* (Herald Press, 2001).

30 See Arnold, *Wildmen, Warriors, and Kings*, 192–93.

31 While the New Testament does not refer to warriors, Paul speaks metaphorically of those engaged in the service of God's kingdom as soldiers (Philippians 2:25; Philemon 1:2; 2 Timothy 2:3). Their sword, however, is God's word (Ephesians 6:17), not cold blades of steel (Matthew 26:52; Luke 22:49–51), as they follow Jesus' way of assertive, nonviolent love.

32 See the shift from nonresistance to the use of force in nonviolent action with Ron Sider, *Christ and Violence* (Herald Press, 1979); Duane Friesen, *Christian Peacemaking and International Conflict: A Realist Pacifist Perspective* (Herald Press, 1986); and John Howard Yoder, *What Would You Do? A Serious Answer to a Standard Question* (Herald Press, 1983), and Yoder's unpublished papers on aikido. For a survey of changes, see Gayle Gerber Koontz, "Peace Theology in Transition: North American Mennonite Peace Studies and Theology 1906–2006," *Mennonite Quarterly Review* 81, no. 1 (January 2007).

33 As Peter Ackerman and Jack DuVall report in their documentary and book,

A Force More Powerful, key nonviolent civil rights leaders in the United States identified themselves as warriors.

34 Mennonite peace activist and founding director of Christian (now Community) Peacemaker Teams Gene Stoltzfus shared with me that he identified himself as a peaceful warrior in the work of CPT.

35 Terry Jones, *The Elder Within: The Source of Mature Masculinity* (BookPartners, 2001), 190.

36 Zalman Schachter-Shalomi, *From Age-Ing to Sage-Ing: A Revolutionary Approach to Growing Older* (Grand Central, 2014), 12. See exercises in the back of his book for nurturing and training the elder within us.

Resources

1 Patrick Arnold, *Wildmen, Warriors, and Kings: Masculine Spirituality and the Bible* (Crossroads, 1991), 94–95.

THE AUTHORS

STEVE THOMAS, MDiv, is the US coordinator for Mennonite Men. A graduate of Hesston College, Goshen College, and Associated Mennonite Biblical Seminary, Steve has served in pastoral ministry for thirty-three years. He cofounded and directed Peacemakers Academy—a Mennonite martial arts school—for ten years, and taught as an adjunct professor in peace, justice, and conflict studies at Goshen College for six years. He is a cofounder of the Indiana/Michigan MALEs chapter of Illuman and a cofounder of Pathways Retreat. He is an ISA Certified Arborist and has a graduate certificate in urban forestry from Oregon State University. He and Linda Lehman Thomas have four children and live in Goshen, Indiana. He enjoys leading retreats, arboriculture, woodland management, furniture making, and being "Poppy" to his grandchildren. Steve's contact information is stevet@mennonitemen.org and 574-202-0048.

DON NEUFELD, MSW, is the Canadian coordinator for Mennonite Men. He has been a social worker for over thirty years, first in child welfare and then (since 2010) in private practice as a therapist. He works primarily with men, addressing a broad range of matters including mental health, fathering, relationships, addictions, and violence. Don has written and spoken about his specific interest in the convergence of clinical and theological thought in relation to men's well-being. He is pursuing a master of theology degree at Conrad Grebel University College. Don enjoys camping, cycling, reading, and working in his yard. He and his wife Gayle live in Virgil, Ontario, and have three sons, two daughters-in-law, and two wonderful grandsons, Rowan and Kayden. Don's contact information is don.neufeld@outlook.com and 905-650-1577.